# A Call
# To Pursue

## Paul Lawrence

Cover design by Joseph Eldredge

Cover Photography by Catherine Lawrence

Set in arial font,

ISBN - 979-8-9882132-7-7

*This book, my first, is dedicated to my Lord and Savior Jesus Christ who rescued me from my most darkest hour and gave my wounded heart a reason to live again. He has never ceased to answer my first two Prayers. "Lord, I want to know the truth", and, "Please, make my life an adventure."*

*This book is also dedicated to my loving wife, Cathy, for her continual support and encouragement and most of all her Godly Patience.*

*Finally, this book is dedicated to my wonderful children, Joshua, Joseph, and Samuel.*

# CONTENTS

# FORWARD

Every human being on the face of the planet has a call to pursue! A call that has come from God Almighty.

Not only is it a calling, like a vocation, but first and foremost, it's a call to seek after Him. That is, after God Himself. Like a parent beckoning a child He has outstretched His hands to all of us, regardless of race, color, and I dare say, even religion. It's a great journey that He has laid out before us, and it all begins by pursuing Him, and in our pursuit of Him, we find our callings. We find our destinies.

This book is about my personal journey of discovery as I myself have pursued that call.

It is what I have come to learn in my own pursuit of God and His calling upon my life. It's my, "Journey to God," memoir. I don't pretend to have all of the answers because, to be quite honest with you, I feel as if I've only just begun myself. Call it, 'step one' of the climb.

Much of what you will read in this book is taken from my own experience. I have come to believe that experience is valuable. That is, experience that is based upon the Word of God, the Holy Bible.

When all is said and done, everything will come down to "knowing" Him. Did you realize that we can do many things for Him, even signs and wonders, but never really "know" Him? Jesus, speaking to His disciples said:

"Not everyone who says to Me, Lord, Lord, ' shall enter the kingdom of heaven, but he who does the will of my Father in heaven. Many will say to me in that day, 'Lord, Lord, have we not prophesied in Your name, cast out demons in your name, and done many wonders in Your name?' And then I will declare to them, 'I never knew you; depart from Me, you who practice lawlessness!" -(Matthew 7: 21-23)-

My prayer is that you will come to truly know Him in a deep way and realize that He has called each of you by name, that He has a great plan for your life, and that you will know what to do when the time comes to do it.

It's your own call to pursue!

As we journey together, may you glean from my meager experience and find the freedom to pursue your own call. May you walk in the adventure of your highest dreams, those God-given dreams. For after the Lord has taken you through the process of change, you too will discover that He has put those dreams there in the first place, albeit refined.

Did you know that there is a ministry within you just waiting to be birthed and announced? There is yet another generation of ministers; servants, who are destined to change the world for His glory and cause more than just you and I to ask, "Why me, who am I that I should have a call to pursue?"

"For the promise is unto you, and to your children, and to all that are afar off, even as many as the Lord our God shall call." - (Acts 2:39) -

... And that is quite a lot!

# Chapter 1

---

## Why Me?

'You have not chosen me, but I have chosen you,
and ordained you, that ye should go... "

- (John 15: 16) - KJV

It seemed to be a night like any other, but I was wrong. I had just returned to the tiny bedroom that I was renting at the back of a house in Santa Barbara, California and was completely exhausted. It was my second year of college, and I was trying to balance an already overloaded schedule. Between attending school full-time, working part-time, and acting in plays the rest of the time, prayer just seemed to be one more task I was falling behind in.

It took all of my strength just to ask the Lord to excuse me from my nightly devotions, something I was always diligent to perform over the two previous years of knowing Him.

Little did I know that I was about to come closer to Him than ever before, or perhaps I should say, He was about to come closer to me!

My living quarter was decorated as an old-English style cottage. There was an oak teacher's desk in one corner, a bookshelf full of antique books against one wall, a twin sized bed beneath two vertical windows, and a tiny closet. That was it! I had to share a bathroom down the hall with another house mate and was granted kitchen privileges. Fortunately, everyone got along very well. It was small yes, but it was home. At least for a season.

Dropping my ever-present burden of books, I undressed and turned off the light. After climbing into bed, the last thing I saw was the bookshelf across the room before I felt as if sleep had literally fallen upon me. Only hours from that moment, and in the direction of where the bookshelf stood, the expanse of heaven would be opened before me... Infinite and eternal... but I'm getting ahead of myself.

It was said by the prophet Joel that God's Spirit would be poured out:

"And it shall come to pass afterward, that I will pour out my spirit upon all flesh, and your sons and your daughters shall prophesy, your old men shall dream dreams, your young men shall see visions: And also upon the savants and upon the handmaids in those days will I pour out my spirit. And I will show wonders in the heavens and in the earth, blood, and fire, and pillars of smoke. The sun shall be turned into darkness, and the moon into blood, before the great and the terrible day of the Lord come. And it shall come to pass, that whosoever shall call on the name of the Lord shall be delivered: for in mount Zion and in Jerusalem shall be deliverance, as the Lord hath said, and in the remnant whom the Lord shall call." - (Joel 2:28-32) - KJV

This portion of scripture was repeated by the Apostle Peter in the book of Acts when the Holy Spirit had come from heaven to empower the believers who were gathered in Jerusalem. Peter, inspired by the Holy Ghost, used this prophecy to describe the strange thing that was occurring on that day so many years ago. (I encourage you to read about it in the Book of Acts, Chapter 2)

I say all of this to predicate what I'm about to tell you, because it must be understood from the scriptures that the Holy Spirit is still with us from the day that He was sent and is still speaking to us today. In fact, Jesus said that He would comfort us and guide us into all truth. I love what Jesus said in John chapter 14...

"If you love Me, keep my commandments. And I will pray to the Father, and He will give you another Helper, that He may abide with you forever the Spirit of Truth, whom the world cannot receive, because it neither sees Him nor knows Him; but you know Him, for He dwells with you and will be in YOU. I will not leave you orphans; I will come to you." - (John 14: 15-18) - KJV

In other words, Jesus said that He Himself would be with us by and through the person of the Holy Spirit, and it was just that person who took me on the greatest journey of revelation that I've ever experienced.

As you continue to read about that fateful night so long ago in the tiny bedroom of my college years, I pray that the Lord would open your ears to hear what the Spirit Himself would say to you.

## The First and Last Star

I will never forget the beautiful music.

Before I could even see where I was, I heard it. It was heavenly music that seemed to be calling me. When I could finally see, I found myself following a narrow trail that made its way up the side of a large mountain. However, it wasn't the trail or the mountain that fascinated me as beautiful as it was. It was the music, the words of which were taken from the book of Revelation which says:

"And the Spirit and the bride say, 'Come!' And let him who hears say, 'Come!' And let him who thirsts come. Whosoever desires, let him take the water of life freely." - (Revelation 22:17) –

Higher and higher I climbed being drawn by the music. Even now, I can still remember the overwhelming feeling of wanting to know the source of it. I wanted to know where it was coming from, and who was playing it. Finally, when the climb up the narrow path was over, I found out.

As I came into a clearing at the top of the mountain, I saw many instruments. There were drums, guitars, trumpets, violins, and many others. Strangely enough, there were no musicians playing them. Just beautiful music pouring forth from them like streams of perfectly blended sound. However, I noticed something unique about each one. They were all broken! The drums were punched through; the violins were stretched beyond repair. Every instrument had something wrong with it and yet, they were still being used of God despite their obvious flaws.

It was a beautiful sight that left me numb, but it was only just the beginning.

After examining the instruments for some time, I began to look around and discovered that I was standing on the top of a lofty mountain. From that great height, I could see long distances. As I began to look over the great expanse before me, I noticed clouds beginning to gather to the north. They were great puffy clouds but rather than being white, they were magnificently colored. Deep crimson reds like blood and fathom-less blues. I saw royal purple as well. As they gathered together, lightning flashed from beneath their folds.

It seemed to be like a great storm racing towards me and the lightning increased more and more as they billowed closer and closer with deep guttural thunder firing sound-bursts like cannons. It was a completely transfixing sight.

However, as the storm came closer, I noticed that it began to part to the left and to the right once again. This was followed by a great calm. Then, in the distance, I saw a star. As far as my eye could see I saw a single star. It seemed further away than any star in our natural galaxy, or even in the universe. It was either the first star of the evening, or the last star of the morning. Perhaps it was both, but before I could even think it suddenly began to rush toward me with a mighty force. And then, in the blink of an eye, He stood there!

Standing before me and drowning out all else was the King of Glory! I knew it was Jesus. That morning and evening Star raced toward me and now stood before me high and lifted up. The mountain top seemed so small then and the music just faded away. I could only hear the sound of rushing wind with cracks of thunder. I stood paralyzed and in awe. Nothing but awe!

His hair was like white lightning, shear and glistening and the robe He wore was of the same. I couldn't see His feet, but I knew that He was standing upon the clouds. This was all perceived through my peripheral vision because

I could not take my eyes off His face. Even if I wanted to, I could not.

It was a face full of faces and eyes. The only way I can describe it in human terms is as if I were to take all the faces of all the peoples that I had ever seen, known or unknown; massive crowds or tiny rooms of people, and place their faces into His, especially the eyes. His face and eyes were the face and eyes of all! It was the most stunning image I had ever seen. As I gazed upon Him, He said not a word, just stood there.

Suddenly, the clouds began to move again. The same clouds I saw earlier began to swirl around until they enveloped me, and as they did, I remember raising my right arm. As soon as it was fully extended... "Whoosh!", I was taken away.

I can still remember the feeling of being pulled through the atmosphere at a tremendous speed. As I was, I also remember looking around me to see if others were coming as well. I thought to myself that surely it must be the rapture. I had heard and read about it, and it certainly felt like it was happening. Faster and faster I raced through the clouds until I heard His voice.

It was a booming voice like thunder. It was as if all the elements sounded forth at once. Fire exploding, oceans crashing, rivers racing!

He said, "I want you to GO!"

After the statement, everything shook in response. All of heaven and earth responded to His voice. Even the heaven of heavens... Even my very soul seemed to shake!

After He spoke, I could feel myself coming back or waking up, one of the two. I felt like Paul in the Bible. "...whether in the body, I cannot tell; or whether out of the body, I cannot tell: God knoweth (2 Cor. 2:3). I can tell you this however, as I was opening my eyes I could literally feel myself hitting the pillow!

When my eyes were fully open, I could see my bookshelf again. The room seemed smaller than ever before. For a moment I laid on my bed in shock, but only for a moment, because when I became fully aware of what had just happened I leaped from my bed and onto my face before the Lord. Almost uncontrollably this happened. As tears poured forth from my eyes, the only words that came to me were, "Why me? Why me?" Over and over again I said them. I couldn't help it, "Why me?"

Why me? I don't know for sure. Why any of us? That's a better question. The Word of God declares...

"But God demonstrates His own love toward us, in that while we were still sinners, Christ died for us. - (Romans 5:8) –

And again...

"For by grace you have been saved through faith, and that not of yourselves; it is the gift of God, not of works, lest anyone should boast" - (Ephesians 2:8-9)-

One thing I do know for sure is that not only are we saved by faith, but we are also called by faith. A call that has come by grace!

A call to pursue!

# Chapter 2

---

## What Now?

"...and bring forth fruit, and that your fruit should
remain: that whatsoever ye shall ask of the Father
in my name, he may give it you."

- (John 15: 16) - KJV

Remember when you were a child
playing in the front or backyard and you heard
your name being called? What was your
response? If you were anything like my
children, you probably just said, "what," and
continued with what you were doing. It wasn't
until the twentieth time or possibly a change of
tone that you actually got up to find out what
that person wanted.

Nevertheless, after that first call,
somewhere in the back of your mind was a
feeling that you were responsible for something.
Responsible to respond even if you did initially
ignore it. Now, imagine that the person calling
you as a child wanted to take you to get your
favorite meal like pizza or ice cream.

Your response would be an enthusiastic one I'm sure! However, many times the thing that we are currently doing, like making mud pies, seems to be more important. That is why we didn't respond right away.

Did you know that God has called each of us in much the same manner? That He's even called us by name? Maybe once or twice. Maybe even twenty times He has called us, but all too often we have been too busy doing what we think is the more important thing. In fact, God has been calling to mankind from the very beginning. Let's look way back to our genesis (beginning) to find out.

"And they heard the sound of the Lord God walking in the garden in the cool of the day, and Adam and his wife hid themselves from the Presence of the Lord God among the trees of the garden. Then the Lord God called to Adam and said to him, 'Where are you?" - (Genesis 3: 8-9) –

Let's take another look at an early account of God's calling:

"Now Moses was tending the flock of Jethro his father-in-law, the Priest of Midian. And he led the flock to the back of the desert, and came to Horeb, the mountain of God. And the Angel of the Lord appeared to him in a flame of fire from the midst of a bush. So he looked, and behold, the bush was burning with fire, but the bush was not consumed. Then Moses said, 'I will now turn aside, and see this great sight, why the bush does not burn. So when the Lord saw that he turned aside to look, God called to him from the midst of the bush, and said, 'Moses, Moses!' And he said, 'Here I am.'" - (Exodus 3: 1-4)

These two portions of scripture give us insight into the "calling" of God. Did you notice how God initiated each encounter? With Adam and Eve, He walked in the garden in the cool of the day. Of course, I'm assuming that God wasn't just out to get some fresh air. Would God Almighty need some fresh air? No, rather, I believe that He was coming to meet and fellowship with His children.

It was the same with Moses. God sent His angel to initiate an encounter with His child. I love Moses' response. He said, "I will now turn aside, and see this great sight." The word "turn" is the key to the calling of God. It means to change course, to redirect one's current path.

Jesus said in the Gospel of Matthew chapter 20 verse 16, "for many be called, but few are chosen." I believe what He meant here is the same as I have been saying. If you look at verse 16 in the entire context of chapter 20, that is, the parable of the workers in the vineyard, you will notice that He paints a picture of God initiating the calling of His people.

One final and important point that I would like to make about God's "calling" to His people is this: Not only has God called us to serve Him, and what privilege it is, but more importantly He has called us unto Him. Meaning, He wants us to experience Him. Experience His presence. He would never have called Himself, "Immanuel," meaning "God-with-Us" if He didn't want us to experience Him. (See Isaiah 7:14). Has He called You? Has He whispered your name?

## Questions, Questions...

Now that we have established the fact that God does call His people, and before we continue with my story, I have a series of questions I would like you to sincerely ask yourself. Better yet, ask the Lord Himself:

- Lord, am I at the right place in my relationship with you?

22

- Am I currently doing what you have called me to do?
- I know that I'm called, but how do I start and what should I expect along the way?
- What's my vision?
- I know my calling so why did everything fall apart?
- There are so many ministries out there, what is going to make this one different?

Did you notice that the series of questions I wanted you to ask were progressive in their contemplation? There is a reason why.

I realize that many of you that are reading this book right now are at different "levels" in your experience with God. Some of you may be just starting out. This may be the first time that you have ever even heard of anything like this. Some of you may have been walking with God for many years. Whatever the case may be the Holy Creator of heaven and earth, God Almighty, has or will tap you on the shoulder to initiate an encounter.

Please don't misunderstand me. I'm not saying that everyone has or should have an overwhelming experience. In fact, Jesus said to His disciple Thomas "Blessed are they that have not seen, and yet believed," (John 20:29) So don't think that if you have not had an "encounter" that you are not called, you are!

If you want one though, ask Him. I pray that He will answer you.

Either way you look at it, you have a call to pursue. Not only are you called to pursue Him, but you have a calling to pursue. Let me say it again. Not only are you called to pursue Him, but you have a calling to pursue.

In your pursuit of Him, you will find your calling. In your calling, you will find your anointing. In your anointing, you will find His glory. In His glory you will be changed, and as you are changed, the world around you will be changed as well. Changed into the image and nature of Jesus the Christ. Changed for His glory!

One day in your pursuit of Him you will touch His heart and His burden will come upon you. It's a burden for the lost and dying. A burden for souls. When that burden does come, what will your response be? If you are serious about your commitment to the Lord, and the time to be serious is now, I'm praying that it will be an enthusiastic one. Just like a child responding to their favorite food.

Look at how the great prophet Isaiah responded when he was called:

"Also I heard the voice of the Lord, saying, 'whom shall I send, and who will go for us?' Then said I, 'Here am I; send me.' And he said, 'Go'. (Isaiah 6: 8-9)

## The Essence of Pursuit

Throughout the years, from the time God said to me, "I want you to go!" I have often wanted to kick myself thinking that I should have asked Him, "How, where, when, and what?" Many times I have been frustrated trying to figure these questions out.

However, throughout the maturing process, I have come to realize that God did not want to tell me at that time. And do you know why? Because it has kept me asking and it has kept me seeking. It has kept me knocking and it has kept me pursuing! It has been a mystery waiting to be discovered, which is the essence of pursuit itself.

Dear friends, even on this day He has taken one step toward you and extended His arms as an invitation to pursue. Take one step, and then another. After that, take some more.

Realize that you too can ask, "why me?" Then journey beyond that to move into the "what now?" phase. Begin pursuing like never before and I guarantee it will be the greatest adventure of your life. It may be difficult at first. I never dreamed of how difficult it would be, but as we continue in my memoirs, I'm sure you will see that it was all worth the price. And it will be for you as well.

# Chapter 3

## Starting Six Feet Under

"He that findeth his life shall lose it: And he that
loseth his life for my sake shall find it."

- (Matthew 10:39) - KJV

"Ladies and gentlemen, the captain has just turned on the seat belt light and has reported that we may be experiencing some air turbulence." So said the flight attendant as we flew over the panhandle of Florida on our way to Orlando.

Looking back at that moment on the airplane, I realize now that the Holy Spirit was probably trying to speak to me through the attendant's voice and if I were hearing with my 'spiritual ears' it should have sounded something like this. "Paul, you may as well get comfortable and strap yourself in because for the next four years you'll be experiencing some mighty shaking in your life while I prepare you for ministry."

With my college years coming to a close, having majored in theatrical arts, I decided to look over my options. It was spring break at Westmont College, and I was spending mine in Florida. Just a few months prior to my vacation I had been given a black and white photo of a model and aspiring actress who lived in Orlando, and she would be the one picking me up from the airport. We had been introduced by a mutual friend named Pauli Shakas who had moved from Santa Barbara to Orlando to attend and pray for the ministry of Pastor Benny Hinn. She rather prophetically told us that we, "just might have a few things in common."

Sure, like how about a lifetime!

I was arriving late in the evening and did not want to burden my spiritual parents, Bob and Johnna Hale, whose house I was staying at, with having to pick me up. Therefore, this model and I arranged for her to do it. After exiting the terminal, I looked around to see if I could see her. One would have thought that I had swallowed a jar full of caterpillars in California and now they were emerging from their cocoons simultaneously...

Then I saw her. It was like God had just parted the Red Sea again because the people crowding the airport became a blur on the left side and the right. Our eyes locked on each other's, and I know we were thinking the same thing: "So this is the one!"

"Cathy?" I asked.

"Paul?" she asked.

"Nice to meet you," we replied at the same time.

If there was ever a conversation loaded with subtext that was it. We spent the next three to four hours together because her car 'happened' to break down on a lonely stretch of road and the nearest phone was a mile-and-a-half from where we were.

I knew in my heart that she was the one God had chosen for me so as we walked, I decided to take a step of faith and unpack the 'baggage' of my life story. I told her how I came to know the Lord, and the miserable mistakes He had forgiven me of. To my surprise this beautiful model, filled with the Holy Spirit, raised in a God-fearing family didn't even flinch. Only smiled.

After dropping off her car from behind a tow truck and borrowing her dad's to take me home, it was three thirty in the morning when we finally arrived at Bob and Johnna's house. Subsequently, we said goodnight and I watched her drive away as a soft and gentle rain began to fall upon me. (A rain whose sweet fragrance I can still smell today). Three days later, at a beach in Long Boat Key, Florida, Cathy and I had a conversation about marriage.

Six months after that we were married.

### No Other Options

I had prayed long and hard for a wife, and when I met Cathy I knew that she was the one, no question. All other options immediately closed. That's just the way it is when you find God's perfect will. The beautiful thing about God's perfect will is the sometimes-hidden strength that comes with it. Difficulties arise, and they always do, but it is comforting to know that there are no other options. It's like Peter's response to Jesus when asked in John, chapter 6, verse 67:

"Then Jesus said to the twelve, 'Do you also want to go away?' But Simon Peter answered Him, 'Lord, to whom shall we go? You have the words of eternal life..." - (John 6:67-68) -

That is what I mean when I say that God's perfect will closes the door on all other options. It may challenge our self-will, but His will is always best.

Jesus said, "He who loses his life for my sake will find it." He was talking about our self-wills and crucifying one's 'self'. For that is where true life, abundant life, all begins.

The book of Jeremiah declares a wonderful promise and a beautiful insight into the heart of God:

"For I know the thoughts that I think toward you, says the Lord, thoughts of peace and not evil, to give you a future and a hope." - (Jeremiah 29: 11) -

If we are going to pursue God and His calling upon our lives, we have to get to the place where we trust Him wholeheartedly.

I'll never forget the phrase I once saw written upon a poster. The picture that accompanied the phrase was of two paths that led in different directions through a thickly wooded forest. One was the high road, and the other was the low. The phrase read, "Never be afraid to trust an unknown future to a known God."

It is what we all have to do when we set out on a journey to follow God, and it is exactly what I had to do when I left California to pursue God in Florida.

## The New World

After spring break, I returned to college and finished out the rest of the year which turned out to be exactly forty days later. At that time, I packed all of my earthly goods into a lily-small Volkswagen Jetta and headed across the United States to Florida. Four days later, I arrived in Orlando, and it felt like reaching an oasis. Not only was the climate naturally moist, but the spiritual climate was as well... Not to mention the prospects of a new wife.

After my initial arrival, it wasn't long before reality began to settle in. I knew that I was going to begin a family in the new and wonderful land I had just arrived in, so finding a job quickly became a priority. However, securing one was another story all together.

One of my original motivations for moving to Florida was to begin an acting career with the eventual goal of working in film. The entertainment industry was on the rise in Orlando, and I thought it preferable to Los Angeles. Besides, studios such as Walt Disney, Universal, and others were in the area. Couple that fact with a pending marriage and I became desperate for work. The only place I knew where it could all possibly happen was in prayer, so I prayed... It wasn't the prayer that changed my life that day as much as it was God's answer to it.

My prayer was a simple one. "Dear Lord," I prayed, "Please open the doors to the studios. I'll do anything. I'll sweep floors and clean toilets if I have to." His response came immediately and simply, and I just knew it was Him. His answer was, "Will you do the same thing for me?"

Many times, God will answer us with a question just as did Jesus so many years ago, and sometimes they can really catch us off guard. In fact, more often than not, His answers will go against what our emotional expectations may be. This usually confirms that it is Him that is speaking.

His question to me certainly opposed my anticipated expectation. I didn't even understand it, but something inside of me bore witness that it was definitely Him. I responded with the only answer I could. "Yes, Lord!"

Then I waited for it to come to pass in the natural.

## Graduate School

The first service that I attended at Orlando Christian Center was an incredible experience. I had previously attended the Benny Hinn Miracle Crusades but had never visited him at his home church. The air was filled with faith and anticipation. Cathy, my future wife, had just landed a job in the Television Department and during services would run one of the five cameras. Therefore, during that first service I sat with my spiritual parents and my soon-to-be father-in-law, Bob Eldredge. Although I hadn't asked his daughter to marry me yet, he knew it intuitively.

As the praise and worship team began to play, the air seemed to buzz with the electricity of God's presence. I had never felt anything like it before and was instantly captivated. However, it was only the beginning. When the praise transformed to worship, eyes that were previously dry wept with joy, including my own.

Waves of God's glory swept over us as angels seemed to walk into the room from all directions. The experience was so real I had to open my eyes just to see if I could see them. As soon as I did, Pastor Benny walked onto the platform from the back room. God's anointing rested upon him so mightily that the entire atmosphere was changed just before he entered, and I could literally feel that change.

From that first service and for the next few years the same thing would happen every time. It was my first lesson in what I have come to call my, "Holy Spirit Graduate School of Ministry." The only way to describe the first "lesson" can be found in the book of Exodus 33, starting at verse 13.

"Now therefore, I pray thee, if I have found grace in thy sight, shew me now thy way, that I may know thee, that I may find grace in thy sight... And he said, 'My Presence shall go with thee, and I will give thee rest." - (Exodus 33: 13-14) -

I could not escape the fact that God had walked onto that platform with Pastor Benny just as with Moses. The experience of God's presence was so real I sat numb listening to the message and wondering how it was possible to walk with the Lord in such a manner. Then I began to "hear" the message and what I heard completely changed my life.

It was a message of death.

Death to self and selfishness. It was a message of the crucifixion and how the cross should be applied to our own lives.

"Jesus said, 'take up your cross and follow me," preached the pastor. "All day long we are killed and counted as sheep for the slaughter," he continued. "Morning, noon, and night we die to self... our own passions... our own wants and desires."

"Dead men don't feel pain. Dead men cannot be persecuted... And God can only anoint a dead man!

The message was shocking, and I'd never heard anything like it. Then the last phrase began to catch up with me and answered the question I was desperate to ask.

"God can only anoint a dead man!"

I suddenly realized how God Almighty, by His Spirit, could walk into a room with a mere man. The man was dead! Dead to self.

By the time the last worship song had played, Benny had left the stage and I just sat in the pew not able to hold back the tears no matter how hard I closed my eyes. I finally opened them, many of the people had already begun to file out of the auditorium. As I stood up to leave, I distinctly heard the voice of the Holy Spirit speak to me. He said, "Welcome home." It was then that I realized that I would be spending a lot of time in that church, but just how much remained to be seen.

## Getting a Job!

During the rest of that week, I tried desperately to find a job, but to no avail. On Wednesday I found myself back at church to bask in the anointing once again. At the end of the service, Pastor Benny released his associate ministers to lay hands on the people and to pray for their needs.

I decided to stand close to watch and learn. I'll never forget when one young man approached one of the associates and said he was desperate for money. He told him that he needed fifty dollars to fix his car. The pastor asked us to stretch our hands toward the young man and pray that God would meet his needs. Able to identify with the young man, I stretched my hands out as well. That's when I heard the voice of the Lord speak to me for the second time at O.C.C., which was a totally new experience for me.

He said, "Give it to him."

"Give what?" I replied.

"Give the fifty and believe!" was God's answer.

I had completely forgotten that I had a fifty-dollar bill in my pocket. It was close to my last amount of money, but I just knew that God was speaking to me in a new and wonderful way. I had no choice but to obey. I walked up to the pastor and handed him the fifty-dollar bill and he looked shocked. After giving the money to the young man he took me aside, gave me a business card, and asked me to call him sometime.

"God is going to use you in this church," he said after handing me the card.

The next day I decided to call him and actually got through, which was a small miracle in itself when you consider how large and busy the church was. As I spoke to him on the phone, I told him about my need for a job. It turned out that the head of the Facilities Department "happened" to be in his office as he was on the phone with me. The pastor asked me to hold on for a moment and I could hear him asking the gentleman if he needed anyone to work. He did, part-time.

By 7:00 am Monday morning, I had already received a uniform, filled out paper-work, gone through security screening, and was ready for my first day on the job. Monday and Tuesday passed fairly quickly as I did odd jobs, but the third day was different.

Very different.

### Definitely NOT in Kansas Anymore

Two young men and I stood with a maintenance supervisor and looked out over the shore of a small lake that the church property was situated upon. It was covered with weeds and eight-foot-high reeds.

"Now, somewhere within 'bout 50 yards of this shoreline is a water pump that used to water the whole landscape on the property. It's stopped up. Gitt this area of swamp cleared out so we can reach it," the supervisor stated.

"How long do you reckon this will take?" asked one of my colleagues.

"It'll probably take about a week... But I have some waders." he jokingly responded.

This is the very reason I entitled this chapter, "Starting Six Feet Under!" This was the beginning of my crucifixion. It took us five days to clear the alligator, snake, and snapping turtle infested swamp. By the time we were done, I was literally "up to my neck" in swamp water and had seen the tail end of a serpent scurrying away.

I grew up in California, and there were certainly no swamps there let alone large snakes, especially in pristine Lake Tahoe. Not even fleas lived in that climate. What I was hearing from the pulpit the Lord was then having me live out, and it had only just begun.

After the first week's task, we were asked to tar the roof of the elementary school which was located on the property as well. It was the middle of summer with 90 to 100 percent humidity. We began the job easily enough, but as the sun began to intensify things got increasingly difficult. At one o'clock in the afternoon the heat became so intense that the tar on my hands began to burn. If that weren't enough, the tar paper itself began to slide off the sides of the objects we were trying to adhere them to.

As each hour passed, our ordeal grew worse and worse. My humility turned to anger. Anger turned to depression, and depression began to deflate my spirit. However, through it all, I sensed a unique closeness to the Lord regardless of the 'death' experience I was going through. With that thought, I tried to persevere... That is, until one more "poke" struck my flesh and popped my tar-covered balloon of determination.

Summer weather in Florida is pretty predictable and what I had to learn the hard way is the fact that rainstorms can, and often do, blow in on a regular basis. At approximately

3:30 in the afternoon, that is exactly what happened.

We had just finished seven and a half hours of laying tar paper on the roof of the school when one such storm blew in with ferocity. Needless to say, within minutes, all of our work was blown over the side of the building. I watched in horror as every ounce of tar paper took a "flying leap."

It took all of my strength not to jump over with it. If I was losing air before, I was totally deflated now. I left work early that day completely miserable and broken.

## How Much Did You Say?

The next day I called in sick so I could "discuss" my future with God. I found some nearby hiking trails and walked as far as I could. In my frustration I forgot to bring water, but it didn't matter at the time because I had business to take care of. It was on those trails that God asked me personally to die to self.

I soon discovered that it's one thing to hear someone preach about the anointing from a pulpit, but quite another to actually pay the price for it. In theory, one would think that many would want to pay the price for the anointing, but in practicality very few actually do. Jesus put it this way:

"Enter by the narrow gate; for wide is the gate and broad is the way that leads to destruction, and there are many who go in by it. Because narrow is the gate and difficult is the way which leads to life, and there are few who find it." - (Matthew 7: 13-14) –

God was asking me if I wanted to pay the price and the narrow walk. Personally, I had just seen the "narrow path" the day before. In fact, the tar of it still burned into my arms and I had to make a choice of whether I was going to follow it or not. It was a fearful thing because scriptures like, "to whom much is given, much is required," came flooding in on me. And, "anyone who puts their hand to the plow and looks back, is not of the kingdom of God." Yet, as I stated earlier, when God shows you His perfect will there simply is no other choice to make...

I sat for hours, no one in sight and just contemplated the "price." Finally, I came to the only reasonable conclusion there was. On my knees in those lonely woods and three thousand miles from where I grew up, I got on my knees before the Lord God of Israel and said, "Yes Lord, I'll do it!"

## My Friend Nathan

What I'm about to tell you is the God's honest truth, and I won't tell you my personal interpretation of the experience. You decide.

No sooner had I prayed, than a man carrying a backpack came walking down the same path I had taken hours earlier. As he neared me, he said hello, at which I returned the salutation.

He then introduced himself as Nathan and told me that he was a "student of the Bible." I told him that I was just praying about my future in the ministry. Then he looked at me and said some very simple, yet profound words. He said, "When you finally get around to preaching, try two different styles. The first time you are in front of a crowd of people, preach at them. The second time you find yourself in front of a crowd, preach to yourself. I guarantee you that the second time will be much more effective."

That was it!

He then opened his backpack, which had at least seven bottles of water in it, and said, "You look like you could use a drink. Here, take a couple of these waters," and handed them to me before leaving in the same direction from which he had come from.

As he walked out of my line of sight, I just stared at the ground contemplating what had just happened. Wondering...

When I finally looked up, a shaft of light was shining through some passing clouds in the exact direction of where Nathan had just walked to.

I went to work the next day with a new determination and new ears to hear the call to pursue. The rest of the summer passed quickly and the new school season started. That was when the maintenance supervisor approached me with a full-time position as the school's janitor. As humiliating as it was, it didn't take long to say "yes" because God had already asked me if I would pay the price and do the same thing for Him.

## Chapter 3: Starting Six Feet Under

The rest of that first year I enjoyed being married to Cathy, my beautiful wife, and tried to enjoy, "doing the same thing for Him..."

I swept floors and cleaned toilets from my new vantage point. Six feet under!

# Chapter 4

## Surviving the Powder Crusher

"And whosoever shall fall on this stone shall be broken: but on whomsoever it shall fall, it will grind him to powder."

- (Matthew 21:44) - KJV

I remember being incredibly nervous my first day at the new job, yet bubbling with excited confidence as I arrived at a building reminiscent of a school. The clothing I wore was a brand-new type of uniform for me. Dress shoes, slacks, a crispy white shirt, and a patterned tie. It was attire I had never previously worn at a workplace and I checked every stitch to make sure I was looking my best for the new boss. I'll never forget opening the door to the reception room and being confronted with an air of reverence. It was really an air of fear, but not in the sense of being scared. It was a fear in the sense of incredible respect. A respect that was certainly not directed at me.

The personnel in the reception room were going about their business in quiet reverence of the man I would soon be working for. He was the principal, and I was hired to be his assistant. After telling the receptionist who I was, I quietly waited in one of the few chairs that decorated the place. I watched the people as they continued about their tasks and pondered who this man must be, and what he was like to command such respect.

After a few moments a door swung open and a strong hand beckoned me to follow, which I cautiously did. I don't even remember looking into his face as I followed because I had been thrown back by an air of authority I had never really felt before. Suddenly, I had a sense of why the other staffers were the way they were. As I followed, I pondered the thoughts and hardly even noticed that we were ascending a flight of stairs that led to the attic of the school.

When the climb was completed the man didn't say anything to me. He only pointed to a spot on the floor where I should stand, which happened to be in front of a large trapdoor. I watched as the principal took a hold of the cord and opened it up. Light immediately flooded the room we were in. When I looked through the door, I found myself at the highest height that I had ever been to.

Chapter 4: Surviving the Powder Crusher

In a conservative estimate, the ground was approximately one thousand feet below me. On the ground itself, rocks, sticks, and barren dirt littered the landscape. Needless to say, it scared me immensely just to look down. With all of my heart I wanted to turn away from that door, but before I could the man spoke.

He said, "You don't know the fear of the Lord!"

With that statement he placed his hand upon my back and pushed me out!

Before falling all the way through, I caught myself on the edges of the door and hung on for dear life.

With a thousand feet of air between me and the ground, fear gripped me like a vice. I could take it no longer, the strong arm of the principal lifted me back onto my feet inside the attic. The last sentence he said to me before pushing me toward a bathroom was, "Now, get yourself cleaned up!" I can still remember washing my hands in that bathroom sink before waking up and realizing that it had only been a dream.

## Back Down to Earth

After fully waking up that morning I felt in my heart that the dream had been given to me from the Lord, but I had no idea what it was supposed to mean. In the natural, I was already working at a job that allowed me to wear a crisp shirt and patterned tie, because after a year as a janitor at the school, and another year as a security officer at the church, I was then working in the Crusade Department wearing... well you know.

In fact, I was just starting my fourth year at the ministry and had already enjoyed three wonderful years of marriage, which included the birth of our first son, Joshua. At the time of the dream, Cathy and I were already expecting our second child. Having already moved into a nice little home and having purchased a new car, my career in the ministry seemed to be blossoming. At least it looked that way externally.

Internally, things were very different.

Something was happening in my heart that no one else knew about. It was something hidden from the outside world that only one person really understood, and that person wasn't even me. It was God. The book of Hebrews declares:

"It is a fearful thing to fall into the hands of the living God." - (Hebrews 10:31) -

Why? Because, speaking about man, God says through Isaiah...

"For I know their works and their thoughts..." (Isaiah 66:18)

And...

"There is no creature hidden from His sight, but all things are naked and open to the eyes of Him to whom we must give account." - (Hebrews 4:13) -

Many of us forget that God knows all of our secrets. Even the dark ones that reside in the attics and crawl spaces of our lives. They are the things that only we know about and sometimes do not understand what they are, or how they even got there in the first place. Those are the things that cause us to act contrary to what God expects of us.

However, those very acts done in secret are laid open before Him, for He dwells in the secret place. Sadly, many have perfected the ability to cover those deeds up falsely thinking that they will never be accountable for them... However, lest you feel condemned, the good news is that God understands them even if we don't. He has an answer to any problem and is willing to patiently work with us once we are willing to expose them to His light.

## Winds of Exposure

I believe that we are living in an hour when God's glory is steadily marching toward us, and that He is about to reveal Himself to us in a way that has never been seen before. However, preceding that great revelation of His glory are what I call, "the winds of exposure."

The natural realm tells us that wind always precedes a storm. Did you know that the wind actually prepares the ground for that soon coming rain? Soil that has been covered for one reason or another needs to be uncovered and cleaned up so that the life-giving water can sink deeply into it and reach the precious seeds below.

This is what John the Baptist did before the arrival of Jesus. He prepared the way of the Lord and made His paths straight. He "cleaned" the place up a bit. The same, "winds of exposure," blew seconds before the coming of the Holy Spirit as well.

## Chapter 4: Surviving the Powder Crusher

"And suddenly there came a sound from heaven as of a mighty wind, and it filled all the house where they were sitting... And they were all filled with the Holy Ghost..." - (Acts 2: 2-4) –

The "winds" are once again blowing upon the face of the earth, and they are here to uncover much that is done in secret. However, these "winds of exposure" are not winds of God's judgment, not yet. The current winds are winds of mercy! They are God's way of mercifully warning us of things to come.

Behind the wind is a storm that is steadily marching toward us. It is the storm of God's glory. I believe that God wants to empower His people like never before, but when the power of His glory fully manifests within us, we will need holiness and the fear of the Lord to sustain it. You see, our mere human bodies; our, "temples of the Holy Ghost," need to be prepared. Amen?

I can only tell you this because I've been through it. During the waning "graduate" years of ministry preparation, the "winds" began to escalate and blow hard upon my heart and life as well.

## Changes in Temperature

Just prior to completing my season at the ministry in Orlando, something began happening in my heart that worried me. A chill began to settle upon my soul.

At first it was subtle, like a slow forming icicle, but as the weeks passed, I became more and more aware of it. It was a phenomenon that became even more pronounced when I attended the church services on Sundays.

If you recall from the previous chapter, the first services and for years afterward were glorious experiences that always left me numb. However, those were subtly changing. A change that had absolutely nothing to do with the services themselves or the ministers that preached. It was a change in my own heart. A change in temperature and it was even beginning to affect my relationship with God.

In fact, Jesus Himself talked about these types of temperature changes in the book of Revelation.

"I know thy works, that thou art neither cold nor hot: I would thou wert cold or hot. So then because thou art lukewarm, and neither cold nor hot, I will spue thee out of my mouth. Because thou sayest, I am rich, and increased with goods, and have need of nothing and knowest not that thou art wretched, and miserable, and poor, and blind, and naked: I counsel thee to buy of me gold hied in the fire, that thou mayest be rich; and white raiment, that thou mayest be clothed, and that the shame of thy nakedness do not appear; and anoint thine eyes with eye-salve, that thou mayest see. As many as I love, I rebuke and chasten: be zealous therefore and repent." - (Revelation 3: 14-19) –

I began to realize that not only had I become lukewarm, but I had come dangerously close to being cold. When the revelation finally began to sink in, I asked myself how it could be. I was involved with a Ministry on the cutting edge of Christianity. On a weekly basis, I saw firsthand as people's bodies were healed and many souls were saved! It was a dilemma that shrouded my own soul in mystery. Then I heard a message from the pulpit that removed the veil of confusion for me...

"Many of you have grown complacent in the presence of God! Week after week you see the power of God displayed with signs and wonders as people are healed and delivered, but you've become comfortable with it. Like Uzza in the Old Testament, the fear of God has ceased to exist. The moment you become comfortable is the moment you become lukewarm!"

It was a sermon that rocked my world, a sermon that exposed my insides. I wrestled with it for a number of weeks, wondering what to do. Finally, in the midst of my struggle, I found myself at the end of my own understanding and felt as though I was poised beneath the shadow of a mighty rock. A stone pillar that was poised and ready to collapse upon me.

I didn't know what to do or where to turn. I became desperate. It was at that point that I decided to pray the most difficult prayer of my entire life. Surprisingly, it was a prayer that was mysteriously within God's perfect will for me... "Father, judge me now lest I be judged later..., when it's too late."

See 1 Cor. 11:31 "For we would judge ourselves, we would not be judged. But when we are judged, we are chastened by the Lord, that we may not be condemned with the world."

With that prayer, the pillar began to fall and its destination was directly on top of me!

## Answered Prayers

Why does it seem as if God answers the hard prayers immediately? Prayers like... Lord, break me! Lord, humble me! Lord, judge me! It's as if He responds with... "Sure, would you like me to use a sledgehammer or a stick of dynamite? I can light the fuse tomorrow."

However, the "bless me" prayers seem to take so long. Prayers like... "Lord, please open this great door of opportunity! Lord, bless my business so I can give financially to your work! Lord, please send me a wife, (or a husband)!" With these, it's as if the Lord says, "Sure, give me forty years... It will happen. No, trust me, it's going to come to pass." Well, that's not always the case but it often seems as though it is.

All joking aside, when I did pray the "judge me" prayer things began to immediately come apart. It was as if I were climbing a great rope and on my way up the "corporate ministry" ladder the rope began to suddenly fray. Stitch by stitch, everything began to fall apart.

To make a long story short, my career that seemed to be blossoming dried on the vine. Our house that we were faithfully paying rent on fell into foreclosure leaving an eviction notice on the door because the owners didn't pay the mortgage. Even the payments on our new car became increasingly difficult to manage.

However, through it all, Cathy and I tried to stick it out, but it became increasingly clear that it was time to move on even though we dreaded the thought.

We, as Christians, serve and follow a living God, and because we serve and follow a living God, seasons of change will always confront us as His people. Like the spiritual forefathers that pursued God before us, our tent poles can, and sometimes must, be pulled up once in a while.

Many times, people don't perceive the change in seasons and stay too long in one place. Meanwhile, the Shepherd has moved on to another. More often than not, this allows bitterness and anger to settle in. That is when we begin to think that other people, circumstances, or "the devil" is the cause of our discomfort when it simply may be that God has moved on and we have not.

I only know this because it happened within my heart. I started to blame others when I should have been following the Shepherd, a mistake that birthed bitterness and further deepened the temperature change in my heart.

Finally, after much contemplation, my wife and I decided to move to California. A move that brought the full weight of the stony pillar upon us. A stony pillar that became the rock that would eventually grind us to powder!

## Entering the Powder Crusher

Knowing that I was called, our first stop in our sojourn was an attempt at a youth pastor position in a mainline denominational church. Therefore, once we applied, we had to wait while a committee of elders made a decision on the applicants. While we waited, my parents were gracious enough to lend us their camper to live in. Even though it was a great blessing, it wasn't the ideal condition for a family of three with another on the way.

Even to this day, Cathy still declares that it was the hardest time of her life. She then found herself three thousand miles from where she grew up and was going through her own, "six feet under," experience. Imagine being seven to eight months with child and trying to wash in a shower half the size of her pregnant belly.

Eventually, the youth pastorship fell through and the old saying, "when God closes a door, He always opens a window," came into play.

Another potential position at a ministry arose shortly after my wife gave birth to our second son, Joseph. Unfortunately, after having packed up all of our things again we were heading through that "window" when it slammed on our fingers. It was yet another blow to the coffin of bitterness I seemed to be decaying in.

With no options left, my parents again extended a hand of blessing by offering their home for us to stay in. We humbly took the offer and tried to stay as quiet as possible which, by the way, is about as hard as trying to quiet down a Florida hurricane, when you have two infant boys to care for. It was a windstorm for sure. A windstorm that continued to blow rain onto the coals of the graying embers of my heart.

## Tomb Time

Have you ever been to a place of being so hurt and broken, even beyond broken, that you didn't even want to pick up the Bible let alone read it? I have, because it was exactly where I found myself after blow upon blow of disappointment came against me.

In the gospel of Matthew there is a powerful statement made by Jesus...

"And whoever falls on this stone will be broken; but on whomsoever it falls, it will grind him to powder."
- (Matthew 21:44) -

In the previous chapter I talked about dying to self and selfishness at the cross of Christ. However, I believe there is a place that we can go to that is even deeper. A place where we are beyond being broken. A place of loneliness where no one else goes. Like Lazarus who died, we go to a tomb that is beyond dying to self. It is utter darkness...

Does this bear witness with you? Have you done any, or are currently doing any "tomb time?" If so, I have good news for you!

## Come Forth!

The place I found myself literally felt like I was being ground down to a powder form. Like wheat beneath an ancient mill stone, I was being crushed to a state of sheer nothingness. And yet, it was a place where God began His most awesome work in my life... And, if you're ready, it is a place where He will begin His most awesome work in your life as well. He began to reveal to me that from that powder form, He could place us, you and me, in His hand and breathe on us by His Spirit to the nations! Why? Because we are light and easily moved. The weight has been removed. Jesus said...

"The wind blows where it wishes, and you hear the sound of it, but cannot tell where it comes from and where it goes. So is everyone who is born of the Spirit." - (John 3:8) -

...And that is good news!

It was only one of the lessons I learned from the powder crusher, but it was a lesson that brought hope into my heart once again. From weeks and weeks of utter despair and darkness, the mere thought that God could actually send me to the nations for His purposes was like a flickering match in my blackened world.

Slowly, very slowly, my heart began to reawaken. However, getting out from underneath the powder crusher was not an easy task. It took a day-to-day walk of faith that began by trying to get back into His world. It wasn't easy by any means, but I tried, nevertheless.

On occasion, when I felt I had the strength to do so, I would flip open my Bible.

Sometimes I would just open it without reading. It was all I could do. However, after weeks of doing that, I recognized a pattern developing. I noticed that every time I opened the Bible it would land on the same page. Was it because my Bible had a crease in it, or was God trying to tell me something?

I really don't know, but one day I gained the courage to begin reading again and was amazed at what I had been opening to all those weeks.

"How lovely is Your tabernacle, O Lord of hosts! My soul longs, yes, even faints for the courts of the Lord; My heart and my flesh cry out for the living God. Even the sparrow has found a home, and the swallow a nest for herself, where she may lay her young. Even Your alters, O Lord of hosts, my God. Blessed are those who dwell in Your house; They will still be praising You. Selah.

Blessed is the man whose strength is in You, whose heart is set on Pilgrimage. As they pass through the valley of Baca, they make it a spring. The rain also covers it with pools. They go from strength to strength. Each one appears before God in Zion. O Lord God of hosts, hear my prayer; Give ear, O God of Jacob. Selah." - (Psalm 84: 1-8) –

I began to see that God was trying to speak to me, but it was still hard to tell what He meant. Finally, after days of reading it and rereading it I began to "hear" the still soft voice of the Holy Spirit once again. A voice that began to gently walk me out of the tomb I had gone into.

## A Still Soft Song

I noticed that the Psalm was really a song written by a songwriter, a fact I hadn't previously known. It was the song of a person who had once known of the glorious presence of God. He knew what it was like to dwell under the shadow of the Almighty, but somehow had lost his way. Like the prodigal son that Jesus talked about, the songwriter was astray. If you follow his thought process, you can see that he has come to the end of himself. A place of utter loneliness. A place of powder....

However, in that place, a revelation comes to the depths of his soul. A soul that longs, yes, even faints for the courts of the Lord!

In verse 9, the songwriter somehow finds the strength to begin the journey back to the heart of God. Back to the heart of worship where disappointment and bitterness doesn't matter anymore. The only thing that matters to him is the refreshing presence of God...

Have you found yourself at that place? A place where the only thing that really matters is the living waters of heaven despite the pain and disappointment? If so, you're ready to take the first step.

Our pilgrim in Psalm 84 then speaks about passing through a place called the valley of Baca, or place of tears and weeping. In Israel, the Valley of Baca was an extremely dry and barren valley. A place symbolic of the wilderness and desperation where perhaps the only water to be had were the tears running down one's face.

However, the psalmist talks about passing through that valley one step at a time. "They go from strength to strength." It's a statement of momentum. In other words, just keep on going one step after another and eventually momentum will build up.

Finally, after patient perseverance the songwriter arrives! With a great sigh of relief he declares, "A day in your courts is better than a thousand days where I used to be! In fact, I'm just happy to be a doorkeeper! Just inside the door is enough for me!" (paraphrased)

Are you at that place of longing? Are you hungry for the truth of God's presence? A truth that burns away all the pain and shame?

Burns away all the disappointment and doubt? All the fear and trembling?

His arms are open to you today. It doesn't matter where you've been or what you've done, or even what has been done to you. "Today, if you will hear His voice..." He's waiting to embrace you at this moment!

Remember, there is a great destiny awaiting you...

"For the gifts and the calling of God are irrevocable." - (Romans 11:29) -

In other words, God has never once changed His mind concerning you. He hasn't even thought of it! My prayer today is that you will have the strength to move beyond the valley of tears and pain, and that you will, as I did, survive the powder crusher. There is still a vision, still a dream, still a plan waiting for you to discover...

Waiting for you to pull it down from heaven to the earth!

# Chapter 5

## Pulling Down D'Vision

"But let him ask in faith, nothing wavering. For he that wavereth is like a wave of the sea driven with the wind and tossed. For let not that man think that he shall receive anything of the Lord. A double-minded man is unstable in all his ways."

- (James 1:6-8) -

After leaving my parents' house at one o'clock in the morning, I drove all night to reach my destination, and arrived only one hour before my scheduled appointment. It was just enough time to shower, change, and make it to a meeting with a manager of the Guest Services Department at a ritzy, five-star hotel on the ocean in Southern California; a meeting that was scheduled only one night before. In my heart, however, I knew that the job would be mine even before they said that they were impressed with my determination to get it.

On a previous trip from the north of the state to the south, Cathy and I had scouted the land that we thought God was leading us to and returned with a good report. The fruit was abundantly favorable!

Even though it was a job parking cars as a valet with co-workers ten years younger than I, I told Cathy that it was a pleasure to do it. After all that we had been through, it was nice to pay the rent on an apartment of our own and an apartment that we knew we could stay at for as long as we wished. I actually enjoyed paying the rent from month to month as our lives began to stabilize and our children started to grow up around us.

Finally, we were once again beginning to live the lives we had dreamed about. Teaching the children how to walk. Watching them graduate from a crib to a "big boy bed." Changing dirty diapers and answering 3:00 am screams... Well, at least it was nice to see them take their first steps. My wife's biological clock had truly been ticking and the alarm had certainly sounded. However, my clock was still waiting for the appointed hour.

## Rebuilding the Walls

Even though the natural walls of our lives were in the process of being rebuilt, I knew that the spiritual ones were still shattered and vulnerable to breach. In the depths of my soul the knowledge that God had called me and had a plan for my life kept me hungry, and that His gifts and the calling of God are irrevocable, (Rom. 1 1:29) kept me thirsty.

Even though I was in the midst of a difficult spiritual recovery, I was encouraged by God's faithfulness to see me through. As the Bible says,...

"Yea, though I walk through the valley of the shadow of death..." - (Psalm 23:4) -

And...

"When they are passing through the valley of Baca make it a well..." - (Psalm 84:6) -

I discovered that along all of our journeys we are to always pass through the valleys, not quit in the midst of them. I turned once again to the only place I knew to start rebuilding. In fact, it was the very same place

75

God started many of His wall building projects throughout history:

Prayer!

## A Welcomed Visitor

I'll never forget the balcony of the little second floor apartment that we lived in. After making the commitment to meet with God every morning, even for just a few minutes to begin with, the balcony was the only kid-free zone in the house.

Imagine what it must have looked like. Two toddler boys just inside the sliding glass door half watching a purple dinosaur on the television and half itching to interrupt dear old dad. And a mother trying to keep them from doing just that, and me huddled under a flowered blanket on chilly winter mornings with headphones like earmuffs on my ears. And still, God was gracious enough to be at every meeting along with His appointed encourager!

Without fail, every morning that I prayed, a dove would come and visit me. It would perch atop the adjacent roof and "coo" the whole time. It was such a unique way for

God to encourage me because He knew that the sound of the dove cooing was, (and still is), one of my favorite sounds in the whole world. It was also His way to encourage me to keep going.

Week after week I met with God and the dove, and slowly the spiritual walls were being rebuilt in my heart. Subsequently, around my family as well. After a time, it got to the point where the peace of God so filled our house that you could literally feel it when you walked in. Cathy and I began to see the scriptures come alive right before our eyes. Scriptures like...

"If anyone loves Me, he will keep My word; and My Father will love him, and We will come to him and make Our home with him." - (John 14:23) -

We learned the secret to having a sanctified home and a place to rest, away from the battles of the world. The scripture that really solidified the concept for us was out of the book of Deuteronomy.

"For the Lord your God walks in the midst of your camp, to deliver you and give your enemies over to you; therefore your camp shall be holy, that He may see no unclean thing among you, and turn away from you." - (Deuteronomy 23:14) -

To illustrate this fact, I'd like to share a story that took place at that time. Before I do, however, let me say that prayer was continually being offered up in our home. When I would leave for my job late in the morning, Cathy would put the kids in for a nap and immediately begin to pray as well. The more we prayed the more God's presence, or in other words, God Himself, would dwell with us.

## The Lingering Presence

One day, Cathy was on her face before the Lord and heard a knock at the door. Not wanting to be interrupted, she refused to answer it. However, the knock persisted until she was compelled to answer. As she did, she was confronted with the face of our next-door neighbor, an unsaved woman struggling to keep her marriage afloat and her only child cared for. In that apartment complex, being on the second floor meant that our front doors literally faced each other, so getting to know the neighbor was an inevitability.

As the woman stood at the door, she asked if she could come in for a while. Cathy asked her if there was any particular reason and she answered by saying, "There's just something about your home that I like... It's, it's so peaceful!"

At that, Cathy let her come inside and she just sat down on the couch without saying a word. My wife thought it to be somewhat strange, but she perceived that the woman was just being drawn by the Spirit of God.

After a few minutes of silence, the woman began to explain to Cathy that she was starting to feel something touching her. In fact, she turned around once or twice while she was talking to see if there was anyone behind her, even though a blank wall was the only thing behind the couch. My wife told her that she was just feeling the presence of God in the house.

At that, the woman got a strange look on her face and left. However, not long after that experience, Cathy led her in the sinner's prayer, and she received Jesus Christ as her Lord and Savior. Praise God!

In the previous chapter, I talked about the psalmist that made his way back to the dwelling places of God. Finally, I myself was rediscovering the glorious tabernacles of the Most High. It felt like being born again... again.

My prayer life continued, but one day the dove no longer showed up on the adjacent roof. It was a relatively short-lived albeit wonderful experience, but God wanted me to move on from there. Like a patient who had completed the healing process in the hospital, it was time for me to leave.

## A Swinging Pendulum

Although our family lives were then stabilized, and my spiritual walk with God was being revitalized, I personally found myself in what I call, "the pendulum effect." Allow me to explain.

Humanity, being what it is, has a tendency to polarize from one extreme to another. For instance, when Moses led the children of Israel out of Egypt, they experienced great signs and wonders of power during their journeys, and it was no doubt the provident hand of God that did so. When they arrived at the mountain of God, or Mount Sinai, they encamped at the base of it.

Moses told them that God was calling him to the top of the mountain to receive the words of the law. That is, the directions of how to relate, follow, and worship as God's very own people. What happened when Moses didn't return for a month and a half? They created for themselves a golden calf. An idol to worship.

It's astonishing how quickly their hearts were turned back to the old ways. Even after physically witnessing how an invisible and living God, not made with wood or stone, was leading and protecting them. Remember the cloud by day and the fire by night?

Yet they swung way back to the side of idolatry like a pendulum. "the pendulum effect." Unfortunately, I was no less guilty of this than the Israelites of old were, for it was exactly what I did with my own calling.

## Decision Time

From before and into the first two years of my experience with God, my life's dream was to become a film actor. I started pursuing that dream in the early years of college before I was saved, and it continued even after the salvation experience. Toward the end of college, I was fortunate to see some rising success on the stage scene. As I mentioned earlier, it was one of the reasons that helped motivate me to move to Orlando, Florida in the first place. Then, after returning from Florida and going through the powder crusher, I found the dream to still be alive. It was like an ember that burned beneath the surface of an ash heap even though things were cool on top.

With no real focus on my personal future, coupled with the fact that my biological clock was ticking, that is, the "what's my career?" clock, I found a deep desire to try and resuscitate the old dream. I mentioned this desire to Cathy, who responded with one of the lonnngggest rolls of the eyes I had ever seen!

After many sighs she graciously, albeit reluctantly, agreed to help me make an attempt at it.

I scouted and enrolled in a few acting for film classes, obtained the necessary headshots (black & white photos), found a commercial agent, and even appeared in two short films. However, on my third shoot, I still hadn't been paid and the pixy dust began to wear off. Volunteer short film acting turned out to be just that, short, and short lived with no pay. I was like a basketball player trying make a basket and not even coming close to the rim, the angelic crowd yelling, "air ball! air ball!"

It wasn't long before I found myself with that empty feeling once again, but I just knew that God had called me to some kind of ministry. But what? Was it acting professionally? Was it preaching? As I told my wife, "If I were to deny that He had appeared to me and called me, I would have to deny that I existed at all!" Only one question remained. Where to find what He wanted me to do with my life? Where did I look?

You guessed it... the prayer closet.

## Life in the Fast Lane

In my desperation for an answer, I made a decision to begin a forty day fast for the very first time in my life. I had read about them and how dangerous they could be, but I also read about how powerful they could be as well. I told my wife the new plan and proceeded with caution. (Just one more reason why I thanked Cathy for her Godly patience on the dedication page of this book!)

The plan was to stick with vegetables and water for a month and a half. You wouldn't believe the combinations and concoctions that we came up with to cook, sauté, stew, and whatever else we could do to make them eatable. We did sort of "mess up" the fast a couple of times by devouring bowls of popcorn, justifying it with... "Corn is a vegetable, isn't it?"

Never mind the pounds of butter and millstones full of salt that accompanied it.

I'm sure God got a laugh out of it because it wasn't perfection He was going to answer. It was the position of our hearts! In fact, even our best attempts couldn't even come close to impressing God. To this day I know He answered my pleas not because it was a perfect fast, although we did go the full forty days, but because it was a broken fast. He loves to answer the broken and contrite cries of the heart.

"The sacrifices of God are a broken spirit: a broken and contrite heart, O God, thou wilt not despise."
- (Psalm 51:17) –

And what an answer it was...

## The Visitation

At or around the fourth week of the fast I had an incredible dream that I will never forget. In it, I was driving my car around and around a building looking for a parking space because cars were already parked bumper to bumper. In prophetic dreams, a vehicle usually represents a ministry because they are what move you forward and they are the things that carry you.

So, in other words, I was trying to find a place for my ministry to fit in, whatever it was. Unfortunately, there were no places to park.

However, as I continued to circle the building, I noticed some benches that lined the sidewalks. To my utter surprise I saw Jesus Himself sitting on one of them. Not in His glorified state like I had first seen Him, but how he would have appeared when he walked the dirt roads of the Holy Land.

Overwhelmed, I stopped my car next to one of the parked cars, left it running, and got out to talk with Him. We sat together for what seemed to be hours as I asked him many questions at which He was gracious and patient enough to answer each one. The funny thing was, I couldn't recall anything that He said in reply... But it was for a reason.

I discovered that the Lord was answering my questions and giving me insight into the ministry that He had called me to do, but the reason I could not recall any of it was because He was speaking it into my spirit. Into my heart and soul, thereby leaving it up to me to discover what He had placed there. Remember, it's a call to pursue! I've seen God do this from time to time and have found perhaps more reasons as well.

Many times, the thing that God calls us to can completely overwhelm us if we see the full picture all at once. Other times, we may try it in our own strength and really mess it up. Either way, it certainly keeps you seeking Him. Just sitting with Jesus was a blessing enough, but our time together had to come to a close.

The one and only thing I did remember Him saying to me was right at the end of our conversation. He pointed to a police car that was driving down the road toward my car and said, "You should move your car before you get a ticket for double-parking."

I replied, "Yes, Lord, you're absolutely right. Will you excuse me?"

At that point, I returned to my car before the policeman reached it. As I sat behind the wheel, Jesus stepped up to the curb between the two parked cars, looked down at the curb, and it supernaturally stretched to make room for me! Then the dream ended.

It was the revelation I had been fasting and praying for. The Lord deposited the idea into my heart which, by the way, turned out to be the first place I had to go and look for it. The visitation prompted me to begin a soul search, and to make a decision about the direction I was to take, for I was "double parked" meaning that I was "double minded."

## My Two Sides

From the time that I was saved there always seemed to be two paths laid out before me. Acting and preaching. Perhaps one of the reasons for it was because I am supposedly related to the famous film actor Spencer Tracy, but I cannot verify that. It's just what I have heard most of my life. Either way, acting has always been an incredible draw upon my heart. However, I knew that I was coming to a crucial time in my life and had to make a wholehearted decision about one or the other. You will never believe where the answer came from and from whom it came by, a cannibalistic native of Papua New Guinea!

For weeks I wrestled in my soul for an answer to my duality dilemma. In my search, I decided to visit some of the top professional acting classes in Hollywood itself, but at the same time attended ministry conferences and meetings always asking the Lord, "Is this it?", or "Is this it?" Finally, I attended a conference in Anaheim, California and the answer became as clear to me as a piece of polished gold. It was at one of Benny Hinn's Partner's Conferences and as I walked into the room, I sensed an exceptional presence of God.

Seeing many of my friends from the ministry was a joy, for it had been a number of years since attending any of the functions. After talking to one in particular, he asked me if he could help me find a seat to which I replied with an enthusiastic "yes." He walked me right down to the second row and seated me at the end and center. That's when I knew that God had something special for me. Not because of the position of the seat, but because of the glory of God that began to touch me. It was the kind of touch that makes the hair on the back of your neck stand on end, and a touch that causes your insides to shake.

After the praise and worship, I found it difficult to even hear what was being said from the pulpit because I was fascinated at what I was feeling. Then, at a pause in the meeting, a video was just beginning to be shown on a television screen. That's when a question bubbled up from within me. I would have to call it an unction of the Holy Spirit because it came not from what I was thinking, but rather the opposite of what my emotional state was at the time.

In my heart, and almost audibly, I began a dialogue with God as the lights dimmed for the video. It was a video that was for the partners who had helped sponsor a Miracle Crusade at a stadium in Papua New Guinea. My dialogue sounded something like this...

"Lord, all of these years I have been pursuing my dream. I've tried to rationalize your calling upon me and have tried to fit it into what "I" want to do, even after knowing the death to self concept..." At the same time that this dialogue, or prayer, was going on within me, the video's introduction was rolling. Continued...

"Lord, please forgive me for trying to manipulate you and for trying to make you conform to my ideas of ministry..." At that point I glanced at the video and started to focus my attention on it, but not before I asked Him one final question...

"Lord, I've been pursuing my own dream and I'm sorry. What I really want to know is... what's your dream? I'd like to pursue your dream for once..."

At that precise moment, an image came onto the screen that God spoke to me through. On it was a man with a small bone through his nose and giant earrings in his ears. He was missing teeth and had bloodshot, yellowish eyes as well, but eyes that were looking up to heaven and streaming with tears. His arms were outstretched as far as they could go, and he was worshiping the one true God. That same God that he was worshipping said to me, "That's my dream!"

Tears flooded my face as the same Lord that the ex-cannibal was worshiping continued to speak to my heart. He said, "I will bless your acting career if you choose to pursue it, but know that it's a silver calling. Make no mistake, I will bless it. However, the preaching of the gospel is my gold calling for you!"

For yet another time in my life I was confronted with a revelation of God's perfect will for my life. I knew that there was only one answer to give. However, before I could give a reply, even as the words were upon my lips, I heard the Lord speak to me again.

He said, "Know this though, gold is refined at a much hotter temperature than silver is."

After contemplating what I had just heard, I replied to Him, "I don't care, Lord. For the rest of my life, I want to pursue your dream. I want to preach the gospel to the multitudes."

## Chapter 5: Pulling Down D'Vision

As I sought Him in the fast and had pulled down the vision from heaven to earth, He placed that vision into my heart. His dream. With the decision I made that night, my double mind and the division was pulled down as well.

# Chapter 6

## Principalities & Practicalities

"For we do not wrestle against flesh and blood, but against Principalities, against Powers, against the rulers of the darkness of this age, against spiritual hosts of wickedness in the heavenly places."

- (Ephesians 6:12) -

It was Father's Day, shortly after my decision to preach the gospel, and the boys and I were looking forward to seeing one of the new animated movies that hit the theaters around that same time every year. As we piled into the minivan, Cathy agreed to drop us off on her way to the shopping mall. Tangible excitement filled the vehicle as the kids rapidly fired questions about the movie at me like machine gun bullets. At which, I bravely held up the shield of "let's just wait and see" for protection.

Upon arrival, those same machine-gun toting toddlers were immediately rolling like tanks to the ticket counter. I have to admit though, the excitement was infectious. So much so, that my wife abandoned her desire to go shopping (I told you it was infectious), and decided to join us.

## The Realities of War

At approximately a quarter of the way into the movie I was suddenly struck with an unusual sense of quietness coming from my youngest son. I happened to glance over at my wife who was holding him on her lap and discovered that they were both desperately fighting off sleep. I asked her if she was all right, and she said that she had felt sick. Very sick.

As I felt her forehead and that of my son's, I soon discovered just how true her statement was. She was not only sick, she felt like her head had been in an oven for over an hour.

Upon our arrival back at home, Cathy immediately went to bed, and I put the kids into theirs. Because of her condition, I decided to spend the night on the couch so that she could get a better night's sleep. To me everything seemed to be somewhat normal, like a regular flu had attacked her, but I was wrong. Dead wrong.

At a quarter after one in the morning I was suddenly awakened out of a deep sleep with the overwhelming sense of having to pray for my wife. After about five minutes of intercession, I heard her go into the bathroom where she began to make moaning sounds of pain. As I arrived to assist her, I was astonished to discover that her face was beet red, and the temperature had seemed to go even higher. On top of that, she was swaying back and forth over the open toilet as if she were going to vomit. I figured in my mind that it would probably have been the best thing for her anyway. However, to my utter shock and horror she looked at me and tried to speak. "I, I don't... I..."

With that, her eyes became fixed, and she slumped backward against the wall. Her face, which was previously red became instantly whitish gray, and the heat of the fever disappeared. I was stunned at her condition and began to call her by name, even shaking her to try and get a response. All I got in return was a lifeless, fix-eyed stare.

My next response was to run to the phone to call the 91 1 emergency number but on my way to do so, I clearly heard the voice of the Lord speaking to me. Actually, it was more like a stern command that froze me in my tracks:

"If you touch that phone, you will never see your wife on this earth again."

For a moment, I felt as though I was frozen in time. What was I to do? With the life of my wife hanging in the balance, I decided to obey God and returned to her side. When I got there, her eyes were still fixed and lifeless. A minute or so had already past, but with no thought of it I wrapped my arms around her and commanded "life" to return to her body in the name of Jesus. There was still no response, so I did it again, louder:

"I command life to come to this body in the name of Jesus!"

At that, she began to moan once again, and once again I heard the voice of the Lord.

"Now, command the spirit of death to leave." I heard Him say.

"You spirit of death, in the name of Jesus Christ of Nazareth, leave this place!" I commanded.

The response was instantaneous and dramatic. With an extremely long and drawn out dry-heave, Cathy doubled over and held her stomach. And then everything was still and quiet.

For a moment I thought she was still in pain, but she looked up at me and said, "It's gone, I'm completely healed... and... and I'm hungry!"

It was true. When I felt her forehead again she felt completely normal. One can only imagine how stunned I was. It was numbing!

As she proceeded to the kitchen for a snack, I slipped into the bedroom to pray. The only thing that I could say to the Lord was, "I don't know what to say." Then I saw a vision and was ministered to by the Holy Spirit.

In the vision I saw a figure dressed all in black, with a black hood over his/her head and heard these words, "It was witchcraft... You see, the enemy knew that if he could derail you now, your ministry would never even get off the ground. Welcome to the realities of this war."

## Demon Seeds

As my wife and I discussed the encounter we soon discerned that Satan was trying to cash in on some seeds, or rather "weeds" he had sown years earlier. Allow me to explain.

Cathy's mother passed away of cancer in the late 1980's. On the day of her death, Cathy and the family were at home. What an excruciating experience it must have been. My wife was actually at the bedside when her mother exhaled her last breath. (She was a believer, so she did go home to be with the Lord.) However, just before she expired, Cathy heard a sinister voice which said, "Take a long look at her, because that will be you one day." Fear seemed to overwhelm her. So much so that she completely fainted.

From that time until the "attack" she was very fearful of dying from cancer. It was the seed that Satan had sown in her young, vulnerable heart. That's just the way he is you know.

Years later, when he saw that she would be moving into the fulfillment of God's plan he tried to reap what was planted before it was too late. Guess what? It was too late! By the power of God, who alone deserves the glory, the seed and Satan's plans were destroyed, and a miracle ministry was conceived.

Shortly after the enemy's attempt to derail our ministry I met a pastor and prophet from Dallas, Texas by the name of Howard Richardson. It was definitely a divine connection and certainly God's timing because I had so many questions about the practicalities of ministry. I must have inundated him with tons of inquiries, but he was gracious enough to answer them all. I was so intrigued to know what went on behind the scenes and was so green to the realities of it all. It was nice to have someone who could "show me the ropes". I always looked forward to his visits to California, and always had more questions to ask when he came.

After a few visits, I finally got the courage to ask him about his church and the possibility of visiting it. I had no idea that the Lord had already spoken to him and told him that I was going to ask. He immediately replied by asking me to come and preach, I was shocked.

Did he also know that I had never even held a microphone in my hand before?

## Bible Belt Preachin'

My wife and I arrived in Dallas and were treated like royalty. We felt like little children trying to wear adult clothing as we somewhat stumbled through our introduction to itinerant ministry. However, Pastor Howard was patient enough to walk us through. Then came the sermon. It was a Sunday morning and the last thing I heard the pastor say to me was, "After a few hours, throw the service back to me and I'll finish it up." A few hours....

In front of ten.... twenty.... three hundred people?!?

It had to have been one of the most boring services in the history of Texas preachin'.

I practically read my sermon to them from my yellow legal pad, along with reading half the Bible as well. However, after almost three hours of preaching, that's right three hours of preaching, I saw tears falling from the eyes of some of the people. Tears of boredom you ask? Perhaps some, but God was gracious enough to fill the room with His presence and touched many of the others.

When the five-hour church service was over, Pastor Howard took me aside and said, "You did a real bang-up job. Good work, but... throw away them notes!"

## 501-C What?

Upon leaving my job at the hotel, God miraculously provided a better one for me through a close friend in the real estate industry named Tim Racich. I had been at it for about a year when my bosses Greg and Jean Metcalf, born again Christians themselves, approached me about incorporating our ministry. I quickly agreed with enthusiasm but had no earthly clue what the process would entail. Fortunately, my father-in-law had already crossed that bridge a number of times and was available to lend my wife and I a hand over it. He helped us with the by-laws, but the vision and purpose were ours alone. I immediately found myself on the road to the prayer closet as the weight of responsibility knocked on my front door. A knock I wasn't quite ready to answer.

The process of discovery began very naturally. In the stillness of the prayer closet I began to reach deeply into my heart to uncover what Jesus had put into it when we talked on the bench together. The first thing I knew was that I and my wife had always had a passion for the presence of God. In other words, our greatest delight was to be in the same room with God because we knew that where He was present, troubles were not. The question however, was how to encapsulate and incorporate that concept into a physically working ministry without trying to "box" God in.

The only word I could come up with to describe what I wanted the ministry to be was the word "breath." To me it felt like a word that described the presence of God without limiting God: Like trying to capture a picture of the wind. Obviously, one cannot take a picture of the wind itself, only the effect it makes on the object(s) it touches.

"Breath" seemed to me to capture that perfectly.

But "Breath" was not enough for a name by itself, so I tried to think of a phrase that rolled, "trippingly off the tongue," as William Shake-speare put it. With further prayer and meditation, the name finally sprang forth from my heart like an uncorked bottle.

"Breath of the Almighty Ministries."

I instantly fell in love with it because it not only described our passion for God's presence, but more importantly, it revealed the secret to ministry itself. That is, the simple fact that the ministry could not function, grow, and bear fruit unless it was by the direct hand of the Lord by the power of the Holy Spirit. In other words, if God didn't carry it Himself, it simply wouldn't be carried at all. Besides, it would have been far too heavy anyway.

A number of weeks afterwards I was in prayer and felt led of the Lord to open my Bible to a certain verse of scripture in the book of Job, and was shocked to discover what it read...

"The Spirit of God hath made me, and the breath of the Almighty hath given me life." - (Job 33:4) - KJV

I never even knew that the phrase existed in the Word of God, but there it was. I was convinced that God was going to bless what we had put our hands to do.

After the revelation of the name became apparent, the rest of the vision fell naturally into place. Cathy and I, along with legal counsel, walked through the process of incorporation for about nine months...

The final sealed certificate of approval for Breath of the Almighty Ministries arrived a few days after my birthday but was actually signed by the Secretary of State of the State of California on December 8, 1999. It was the day I turned thirty years old! The same age at which Jesus began His earthly ministry as well.

## Jumping the Gun

Cathy and I were so excited about our ministry and being ministers, even though my speaking engagements were few and far between. (Okay, they were basically non-existent). However, I knew that I was finally on the course that God had chartered for my life. Simply put, the boat was built and ready to hit the open seas. Unfortunately, I didn't pay much attention to the fact that the boat was still in the harbor, and that there was still quite a distance to travel before hitting those open seas.

We thought we heard the sound of the starting gun, but perhaps it was just the sound of the christening bottle breaking on the bow of the ship as it rolled off of its dry dock trailer. With that "sound" I decided to take a step of faith and quit my job to pursue preaching on a full-time basis. As you will see, we must have looked pretty silly racing a boat that was only sitting in the safety of the harbor.

## Mistake, or not Mistake, that is the Question...

My spiritual mother, Johnna Hale once said to me that there were no mistakes in the kingdom of God. Although it was a hard phrase to swallow at the time, I still believe it to be true. Remember what the Lord said through the prophet Isaiah?

"For My thoughts are not your thoughts, nor are your ways My ways', saith the Lord. 'For as the heavens are higher than the earth, so are My ways higher than your ways, and My thoughts than your thoughts. - (Isaiah 55: 8-9) -

And the apostle Paul:

"... we know that all things work together for good to those who love God, to those who are the called according to His purpose." - (Romans 8: 28) –

Even now, as I think back over our pre-launch days, I see it not so much as a mistake but as further preparation. (Isn't time a wonderful thing?) As my wife, children, and myself walked through our experience it seemed to look like a disaster, but was it really?

After leaving the job, the first task I gave myself to do was to spend my mornings in prayer. For four to five hours a day I did just that, and for a total of fifty days I experienced a glorious time in the presence of the Lord. As a full-time minister I just figured that it was part of the job. During that time, the vision and purpose of our ministry became clearer as God revealed His desire for us to reach out to the ends of the earth and... "To circle the globe with the restorative power and presence of God."

How was I to know that it was a long-term goal? It's funny how mountain peaks always seem to look closer than they actually are. Within no time, we were on the radio all over Europe via short-wave frequency through an incredible ministry called, "High Adventure Ministries." Not only that, but we immediately began sending copies of our ministry magazine, a home-grown publication called, "Breath of Life," to our entire mailing list. In addition, we began holding monthly meetings in Southern California and even started a program to help the homeless and hungry. All of which was wonderful ministry work.

However, as we were touching the world with the gospel, our own personal resources waned leaner and leaner along with our stomachs and waistlines.

It wasn't long before we had to leave our apartment to "hit the open road". That was when our troubles really began!

We instantly became homeless and started drifting aimlessly throughout Southern California, looking for a place to get plugged back in. Imagine a premature baby gasping for air because its lungs are not yet fully developed and you can get the picture of where we were as a ministry and as a family. One can only imagine the confusion and disillusionment we were going through.

There the questions arose...

Did my faith begin to waver like Peter's did as he stood on the water at the word of the Lord, or had I taken a step of presumption? Had the "substance of faith " dropped into my spirit, or was I still in a state of hope? (See Heb 11:1)

It was a mystery I didn't know then, and to I to be quite honest, still don't know to this day. However, I do know that it will be one of the first questions I ask when I get to Heaven.

## Rock Bottom

After a few days of wandering, we found ourselves on a hot summer day in Malibu underneath a lifeguard stand with hundreds of people enjoying the beach completely oblivious to the extreme trial we were in the midst of. The turning point came from the mouth of my youngest son, Joseph, who appeared to be trying to hold back tears...

"Dad, can we go home now?" he naively asked.

"Well son, we don't have a h..."

It was the breaking point for me. Right there on the beach I asked the Lord to forgive me for any mistake I may have made and asked Him to help me make things right for the family and the ministry.

As humbling as it was, I took the first step in a long and arduous journey back to where we had started by returning to my former bosses and asking them for my job back.

They were kind enough to let me begin again and even assisted us in our housing situation as well. Once again, Cathy and I found ourselves having to rebuild from scratch.

Metaphorically speaking once again, it was as if we had launched our ship and before we had even left the harbor, a hurricane struck and scattered our belongings to the four winds. I wish that I could tell you that we launched out in faith and the Lord miraculously provided everything by supernatural acts, but I can't... Or can I?

Although everything seemed to evolve back into place naturally, there was no doubting the fact that it was the provident hand of God which allowed us to survive at all. I suppose the whole thing can be compared to the breaking of a bone. Did you know that once a bone is broken, it grows back stronger than it originally was? It's the body's miraculous way of naturally healing itself. I believe we became stronger for our breaking.

Stronger and more balanced.

All in all, I learned some extremely valuable lessons throughout the entire ordeal. One of the greatest was the revelation that the kingdom of God was just that. A kingdom! A kingdom ruled by a king, the King, and a Kingdom ruled with perfect order. Being raised in a free and democratic society, and thank God

I was, dependency can be a difficult lesson to learn sometimes.

Cathy and I started in the ministry seeing firsthand the realities of the principalities that we were up against, but we also had to see the sometimes-harsh practicalities as well. Therefore, I almost hesitate to admit that any of it was a mistake, not because of pride, but because I now clearly see the good that came forth from our pre-launch.

It is all a great mystery, and yet, the pre-launch period was not the final lesson we had to learn. There was yet another sailing exercise we had to go through before hitting the open seas. That was the lesson of, "how to, and how not to, captain a ship."

# Chapter 7

## It's All About... Time!

"Then Jesus said unto them, 'My time is not yet
come, but your time is always ready... You go up to
the feast. I am not yet going up to this feast, for my
time has not yet fully come.'"

- (John 7: 6-8) -

The Greek poet Hesiod, a shepherd
himself once said, "Observe due measure, for
right timing is in all things the most important
factor." In other words, "timing is everything",
and I have found it to be a truth. In fact, it is a
truth that could have only come from the
wisdom of many successes and failures, time
and time again. Successes and failures that came
from all manner of humans throughout history.
For Christians, that is, followers of Christ, it is a
step of faith that we all must take. An entrusting
of our lives not to some twist of fate or the
whims of imaginary gods or goddesses, but to an
omnipotent, omnipresent, and sovereign living
God. The only, the living God!

Faith, that living entity which is a breathing, active, and growing reality for each one of us has a little-known companion. The companion's name is timing. The book of Hebrews states:

"But, beloved, we are confident of better things concerning you, yes, things that accompany salvation, though we speak in this manner. For God is not unjust to forget your work and labor of love which you have shown toward His name in that you have ministered to the saints, and do minister. And we desire that each of you show the same diligence to the full assurance of hope until the end, that you do not become sluggish, but imitate those who through faith and Patience inherit the Promises. - (Hebrews 6: 9-12) -

$F2 + T2 = P$ In a phrase, God's Faith plus our Faith, coupled with and connected to our patient Timing, equals Perfect Power. It was an elusive equation that Cathy and I had stumbled across and were not yet sure how to solve. An equation we had to discover the hard way with a solution we could only solve through much difficulty.

## Bail, Bail!

When I was growing up on the shores of Lake Tahoe in Northern California, I worked a number of summers at a local marina. One of the tasks that I had to perform included the rental of small motorboats to the many families that flocked to the lake every boating season. We had so many boats that each night as we closed, we had to pull them from the water and stack them on boat trees for the night. After a full day of service, each craft would contain bilge water that had gathered on the bottom. Therefore, pulling the drainage plug was an essential step in the entire process. Consequently, every new morning the procedure would be reversed as new families requested rentals.

Occasionally some of the boats, with the families still in them, would begin to sink after an hour or so because someone forgot to put the plug back into the stern of the boat when it was launched that morning. (Whoops, that was me!) Supplying each boat with an emergency distress radio was certainly a stroke of genius. (I wonder who thought of that? Probably someone who had made the same mistake a number of times himself.)

I can still remember my stepdad, Johnnie, who was also the Harbor Master at the marina giving me the "look" as he launched his own boat called the, Welcome Sight, to rescue the stranded people. I would shrug my shoulders, he would say, "hop on," and off we went on another rescue mission. More than once we would arrive on the scene to see the wife and the kids bailing out the bottom of the boat with the dad trying to start an already flooded engine... And the expressions were always the same. The wife and kids with relieved looks on their faces, and the dad bothered by our arrival because he "just knew only a few more tries would get it."

I say all of this to say that Cathy and I found ourselves in a similar situation as our own "boating trip" continued.

### Deep Sea Fishin'

After barely surviving the race around the harbor, the S.S. Breath of the Almighty, or B.O.A.M., finally headed out to open seas. We were chartered for the deep waters where the fish ran in schools of thousands. In fact, it was a small hotel right across the street from one of the world's largest family-oriented amusement parks, Disneyland!

I had taken my time to find just the right room to meet in. The lobby was beautifully decorated with marble and chandeliers, yet it was affordable enough to adhere to our no debt ideals. We planned to meet on a monthly basis with the idea of it growing by word of mouth.

They were some of the most wonderful times I had ever experienced to that point with some of the most wonderful people I had ever met. Adding a new mist to the typical evangelical meeting, which we called, "miracle services," was an after-meeting buffet style dinner. It was a wonderful chance for everyone to fellowship together, and to get to know each other as well.

Above everything else was that fact that God was present with us. It was there that many times I felt led to preach, or rather teach, about the presence of God. It was also there that I learned the difference between the presence of God and the anointing of God, a fact I had not previously been aware of.

## Presence or Anointing?

The basis for the teaching came from a powerful statement that Jesus Himself made to His disciples. It's found in the gospel of Matthew...

"Not everyone who says to me, 'Lord, Lord', shall enter the kingdom of heaven, but he who does the will of My Father in heaven. Many will say to Me in that day, Lord, Lord, have we not prophesied in Your name, and done many wonders in Your name?' And then I will declare to them, 'I never knew you; depart from Me, you who practice lawlessness."

- (Matthew 7: 21-23) -

I have found this portion of scripture to be one of the most shocking statements that Jesus ever made. What He said that was so amazing was the fact that many would come to Him in the end and profess that they had done many things for Him, even miracles in His name, but He would respond by telling them that they never even knew Him.

In other words, just because someone is anointed does not necessarily mean they walk with the Lord. Therefore, knowing His presence, abiding with Him and being in the same room with Him was, and is, much more important than just serving Him.

The danger that I found as I started ministering lay in the fact that God would clothe me with His anointing and authority for each service, like Jacob clothed Joseph, but a few days after the meeting I would be back to face day to day living and the "garment of light" would then lift off me. That was the time when it was so crucial to practice the presence of God. It was a fact that I tried to teach the people who were coming to the meetings as well because I knew that they were experiencing the same thing.

It was during those days that my wife and I made it our passion, and the passion of our ministry, *to dwell with the Lord always...* "To abide under the shadow of the Almighty." (Psalm 91: l) To not just settle for great services, but to see lives changed, including our own. The days when there were no services. The Mondays, Tuesdays, Thursdays, Fridays, and Saturdays of our lives.

Many were touched by God and my belief was that many were changed as well. Not by my teaching and man's wisdom, but by the presence of God Himself. Like Peter and John when the religious leaders perceived, "that they

119

had been with Jesus." (Acts 4: 13) That was our goal.

## Opportunity Knocks

As we continued to minister, an opportunity arose that was not necessarily the perfect will of God but seemed like the right thing to do. Hence the difficulty, or as Shakespeare put it in Hamlet, "Aye, there's the rub." It was where the "bilge-water plug" was loosened on the B.O.A.M. boat.

The chance to meet in another man's church building on a weekly basis presented itself to us, and because we seemed to be ministering to the same people month after month, we thought it only natural to begin meeting regularly. In other words, we started a church. At the same time that the opportunity arose, family members who were missionaries arrived in California from overseas. We were all very excited because it seemed to be the perfect answer to our need of taking the next step in our callings with God.

Therefore, the S.S. B.O.A.M. pulled back from the deep waters and gained some crew members. I, as the captain, decided to head straight into the wind by setting sail for the shallower waters in an attempt to help fish grow rather than just catch them into the net.

We called the church, "Breath of Life Christian Center", and proceeded to enact all of the proper elements including the hiring of a worship director, ordaining the family as assistant pastors, and initiating a team of intercessors. Week after week things began to grow and prosper as we slowly inched forward through the headwind. However, in my private captain's quarters I wrestled with an uneasy and sinking feeling in my heart... And try as I might, I just could not put my finger on the particular problem.

## Le Motif

The way in which I pictured our ministry to be was one in which the world could be reached through. I spent many hours in prayer planning strategies to go to the nations. We started a magazine, a web site, and even took out a D.B.A., (doing business as), for a film production company. I began to see the people as a cooperating team rather than a flock to be shepherded.

As I looked into their eyes week after week, I saw the many wounds that they had come to be nursed of. Wounds that had been inflicted upon them for one reason or another. However, instead of wanting to gently bandage them I often got frustrated because it was something I didn't really want to do. Didn't they know that we had places to go and people to see? Nations to be reached?

The dichotomy began to tear at the seams of my soul, and I slowly began to realize that being the pastor of a church encompassed a much larger picture than I had imagined. It was a much greater endeavor than just creating a programmed machine to reach the masses with.

At the same time, Cathy and I, our family members, and our volunteer staff continued to blow with all of our effort and strength on the sails of the vessel we were entrusted to navigate. At one point, I invited an old and trusted friend, Pastor Howard Richardson from Dallas, Texas. Finally, it was my chance to repay him for the kindness he had shown Cathy and I years earlier.

Our first guest speaker, and the house was packed almost to capacity. When I arrived at the church, I was stunned to see so many people waiting for the word of God and the moving of the Spirit... And God did not disappoint. Following the preaching of the Word, the prophetic gift of ministry flowed like a river throughout the building. When it was over, so many people were touched by God that the air buzzed with excitement and anticipation of things to come. I myself was excited about the sudden growth as many of the visitors said they were looking forward to coming back again and again.

My first impulse was to begin greater planning for the many programs that would surely spring up overnight. However, in the deep reaches of my soul there was still that nagging feeling that I couldn't quite put my finger upon.

To be quite honest, it was like a desperate feeling of having to care for and shepherd so many at once, but at the same time move them toward the goals we had as a ministry. I felt compelled to organize a team to reach the world, but I didn't want to deal with their pain and their hurts. I even wanted to avoid those hurts and even more so when I discovered that there would be many more to deal with as the church grew. Was that the heart of a pastor?

After the formalities, we blessed and thanked our friend for all that he had done to help us move forward and then retired for the night. For me, it was a restless night spent agonizing over my upcoming week. (I was still working a full-time job in real estate.)

Approximately midway through the week I found myself in my private captain's quarters, the prayer closet, and on my face ready to release another of those "hard prayers" to heaven. It was a hard prayer because I knew that it would be answered quickly if it was truly **the** Holy Spirit convicting me to pray it. It was also hard because in the natural word everything seemed to be blossoming. Still, we were on the edge of total commitment to the idea of having a church, but had not yet gone over it. It was precisely at that "edge" where I had to confront that "feeling." Something was amiss.

With gut-level honesty I laid my heart before the Lord knowing that I wasn't being quite honest with myself and consequently, the precious people who would soon be under my care. A fact I knew I couldn't hide from God either. Did I only want the people to come so that we could build a worldwide ministry?

"Hmm." (I prayed) "Lord, if this is not the right season for me to be a pastor, if this is not your perfect for my life right now, then I ask you to shut the door and slam it so that it's very clear... Amen, I think."

## The Ship was Sunk

I've seen boats fill with water, but never have I seen a ship so overwhelmed with it at once. Perhaps in "Titanic", but even that took a little bit of time! The very next Sunday we had three people in the pews. Three! From about one hundred and fifty a week earlier to three! We had more people in the worship team than we had in the pews even if we did ask those few to take up a couple of chairs apiece. God had answered my prayer. Remember what I said about the hard prayers? It's the reason I still say it to this day. It was a crystal clear, immediate answer.

Not only did I discover that the plug had broken free from the stern of the ship, but the whole back end of the boat fell apart. Which, by the way, was the traditional location of the captains quarters on the old Spanish galleons, frigates, and sloops.

In a very short time my immediate family, our extended family, and our volunteer staff found ourselves each floating on broken planks with only the shirts on our backs, (figuratively speaking.) Planks that eventually drifted in separate directions. As each of us continued on our own personal journeys with God, by grace we carefully nursed relationships back to health.

I realize that this all sounds like a tremendous tragedy, but it was not. It was simply the powerful hand of God working through our choices to adhere to His perfect will. A will we all knew to be the best in the end. Remember, we are called by faith and not by sight. If faith is the life that God wants us to live, then wouldn't it make sense for Him to give us the leeway to make a few would-be mistakes? Thank the Lord that He does because...

"We know that all things, (not just some things), work together for good to those who love God, (and desire His perfect will), to those who are the called according to His purpose."

- (Romans 8-28) (parenthesis mine)

I have come to believe that miracles are born through pain and suffering, and no one can testify to it more than someone who has been through the fires. Did you know that anyone with a *message* has only experienced a *mess* over time; a mess with age? Our third child came into this world in much the same way.

Cathy and I had been believing God for another child to add to our previous two, but after back-to-back miscarriages we questioned whether it was possible at all. It was a striking similarity to our ministry itself. Two children and two attempts at seeing God's will manifest in the earth were cut short. However, we refused to give up. Like the pilgrims who sailed over halfway across the mighty Atlantic Ocean to bring birth to a new nation and a new freedom in God, we had come too far to turn back. The only choice left was to press on and persevere.

Cathy, being a descendant of one of the original Mayflower pilgrims herself, found the strength within her body to bring forth our third child. A healthy and happy son named Samuel Josiah Lawrence was born. He was our third attempt at childbirth and became our third child after three tries. I like to call him a child of the third day. In other words, a child of the resurrection. Consequently, his birth gave us the courage to believe that things were going to change in our ministry as well if we were to give it just one more try.

A third try!

## It is About Time!

As I diligently continued to study the scriptures without giving up, I found one that leapt off the page one day.

"John came baptizing in the wilderness and preaching a baptism of repentance for the remission of sins. Then all the land of Judea, and those from Jerusalem, went out to him and were all baptized by him in the Jordan River, confessing their sins."

- (Mark 1: 4-5) -

When the scripture said that all the land of Judea, and those from Jerusalem responded, I knew there was something more to the work of ministry. The revelation lay in the fact that God had a timing for His work to be accomplished. It was by the Spirit of God that all of Judea and Jerusalem responded to John's ministry. I realized that he didn't send out flyers and pour through the local phone books to get the people to respond. It was simply the work of the Holy Spirit at the God appointed hour.

I also realized that when we had launched out the first time it was by faith, yes, but not through patience. Remember the elusive formula? (F2 + T2 = P7). The second

128

time it was by our own strength and good ideas. In other words, it just "seemed" like the right thing to do.

Just picture it, there we were on the bow of the ship trying to blow the sails forward, even contrary to the wind for that matter. Wouldn't it have been much easier to just turn the boat and let the ocean breezes, the Breath of the Almighty, blow the ship to its pre-charted destination?

Therefore, I made the decision to shut down all of our efforts at ministry and to sit and wait... While we waited we drifted on simple planks of wood, and while we drifted, I enjoyed not constantly having to repair the gaping holes anymore and plug the ever leaking hull. The planks themselves were very low maintenance, and simply kept us floating.

## Drifting for God

Drifting was not necessarily a bad thing. It was the "let go and let God" concept in action and a time to release everything to Him. While it was in His hands, He did an amazing thing with it.

Shortly after closing the doors on Breath of Life Christian Center, a brand-new opportunity opened up and I knew with all of my heart that it was God's idea and not my own that time. In fact, He had spoken it to me years earlier in a dream. It was my very first prophetic dream, and I had nearly forgotten it until the day that it came to pass.

I was invited to attend a bible study at the home of a Grammy Award winning musician by the name of Jamie Jones. He and his wife Hannah had just started the meetings in an attempt to grow closer to God and to experience the deeper waters of His presence and Word. My good friend Pastor Howard Richardson conducted the meeting, and the glory of God really filled the room.

I myself was bubbling inside. As we all had fellowship together at the end, the remembrance of the dream came flooding in on me and I could not contain it. I had to pour it out, for it had been in my spirit for ten years.

When I told the dream, I knew it was the fulfillment of the ten-year-old prophecy...

## The Narrow Path

It was the early nineties, I was twenty-one, and was scheduled to attend a special dinner hosted by a man I had been working with in the film industry. The dinner was to celebrate my promotion within his company. I had just recently given my life to Christ but was excited about fulfilling my lifelong dream of working in film. However, the night before the dinner, the Lord gave me a warning. A dream that shook me to the core. (It must have been the way Joseph felt when he was warned in a dream to flee to Egypt with the baby Jesus and the child's mother, Mary)

In the dream, I found myself walking up a long and wide driveway that led to a Hollywood party.

I knew it was a Hollywood party because I could see executives and celebrities talking and laughing together. Needless to say, I was excited to be going.

Lining the driveways on both sides were a series of telephone poles upon which giant red owls were perched. As I neared them and began to cross their line of sight, they started to swoop down and dig their talons into my head. Each subsequent step I took, another would do the same.

In my heart, I knew that I couldn't continue on the wide road and still survive so I began to look for an alternate route. I was surprised to see a narrow trail that led into the woods on my right. With no other real choice, I began to follow it.

The narrow trail took me over trees and past waterfalls. Down gorges and over hills, but I kept following it for as long as I could. Finally, after a very long journey, I came to the end and was shocked to see where it had led me. After so much time, I found myself at the Hollywood party that I had originally been heading to! The only thing I could say to the people was how wonderful Jesus was, and what He was really like. In other words, after trusting God's calling upon me and not my own, and after much preparation, I was preaching in Hollywood!

### Our Lives in His Hands

The dream had come to me before I was even called. Before my mountain top experience that started this book. It came before I met and married my Cathy. It came before we had our kids, long before. It even came long before I ever dreamed of being the president of a ministry called, "Breath of the Almighty" But God knew the beginning from the end. Like the book of Hebrews says about who Jesus really is... "The author and finisher of our faith..." (Heb. 12:2)

Why did the dream come? To warn me yes, but also to be a "road marker" on my journey with Him... And even though I had stumbled along at times, I knew I was still on the trail the day it came to pass.

Just like the dream, the journey so far has been a long one full of and turns. It's gone over obstacles, into dark valleys, but also past beautiful sights like majestic waterfalls. One thing it has not been though, and that is wide. It has never ceased to be *a narrow walk.*

Shortly after my first visit to the Hollywood bible study, I was asked to speak and to minister myself on a monthly basis. At the time of this we were still holding those meetings in Hollywood. Not because we were anything special, but because God ordained it from the foundation of the world. A world that He still loves and still wants to touch. As my wife says, "When you touch Hollywood, you touch the world."

A Call to Pursue

My journey with God has been an incredible adventure so far, and yet the scripture which says...

"Eye has not seen, nor ear heard, nor have entered into the heart of man the things which God has Prepared for those who love Him."

- (1 Corinthians 2:9) -

has still more contained within it not only for me, but for you as well. There is yet another generation of ministries just waiting to be birthed and announced to the world.

Will yours be one of them? Will your business, your creative ability, or whatever your calling is, be one of them? That's up to you. It only takes your willingness, because God Almighty has more for you. He always has more!

I can almost hear Him asking... "How high? ... How far? ... How fast?... Because I'm ready if you are!

Are you ready?

# Chapter 8

## New Generation Ministries

"Thus saith the Lord which maketh a way in the
sea, and apath in the mighty waters... Remember ye
not the former things, neither consider the things
of old. Behold, I will do a new thing, now it shall
sping forth, shall ye not know it? I will even make a
way in the wilderness, and livers in the desert."

- (Isaiah 43: 16-19) -

From humble beginnings Jesus was
born on this earth, and it took much humility to
lay down the glorious position He once had. It
took humility to condescend to the level of a
filthy almost forgotten feeding trough, the
manger. It also took humility to willingly subject
Himself to His earthly parents until the fullness
of His time was appointed and then announced
by the Father... And it took humility to patiently
wait for His inheritance. What was that
inheritance?

The earth's vineyard of souls from
yesterday, today, and forever! His family.

Did you realize that every child of God has an inheritance as well? Would not the Father, whose glory fills the earth, reserve for each one of His children an inheritance for them to receive? Peter put it this way...

"Blessed be the God and Father of our Lord Jesus Christ, who according to His abundant mercy has begotten us again to a living hope through the resurrection of Jesus Christ from the dead, to an inheritance incorruptible and undefiled and that does not fade away, reserved in heaven for you, who are kept by the power of God through faith for salvation ready to be revealed in the last time."

- (1 Peter 1: 3-5) -

You may have come from a poor family or broken backgrounds. You may have come from the worst possible scenario imaginable..., but you have an inheritance! You may have come from a wealthy background with all the best that this life has to offer. You may have fame and fortune..., but you have an inheritance! You may live in a country where ninety percent of the population is starving or is infected with the HIV virus. It may even be a country that does not even believe there is a God, that God is dead..., but you have an inheritance!

The inheritance we all have is not a material inheritance, although material wealth may be a symptom of it; but they would be just that, a symptom... No, the real inheritance is a spiritual vineyard.

Each one of us has a plot of land within the realm of the kingdom of God. In other words, once we voluntarily become children in the family of God, we instantly become heirs as well. Heirs to the family fortune. What is that family fortune? A spiritual plot of land that only we can tend and tending it will be required because we are "called" to do so.

Within the tending and cultivation, the blood, sweat, and tears, are contained the sweet grapes of God's new wine. Imagine if you were to receive a natural plot of land that contained a vineyard upon it. Now imagine the vineyard to be overgrown with weeds and thorn bushes. What would it take to cause that vineyard to produce fruit? It would take a mighty pair of clippers, perhaps even a machete' to start with. (Spiritually speaking, this would be symbolic of the Word of God.) It would take irrigation and a constant flow of water to nourish the soil. (Symbolic of the Holy Spirit.)

Speaking of soil, it would have to be broken up and loosened so the water could filter into it, (soil being symbolic of each of our souls.)

And that is where our inheritance lies, deep within our own souls. Our soul is the soil where God Himself has placed His deposit. His seed. The seed of His Son's inheritance was sown in the souls of human beings when we were created and only the Son Himself, entering into each soul through faith, can crack open each seed.

The question has been asked, "Has God ever created a rock that He Himself could not lift?" The answer is, yes. Your heart... Your will, is that rock! I encourage you to surrender your will, that rock to God today and He will use it to crack open the seed of new birth and life.

He will then open the door to the inheritance reserved for you. A life full of the new wine of God's Spirit. Now is the hour to pursue Him and that wholeheartedly. Now is the hour to pursue His calling for you and remember, in your pursuit of Him, you find your calling.

## Carriers of Glory

"And when they came to Nachon 's threshing floor (the place of preparation), Uzzah put out his hand to the ark of God and took hold of it, for the oxen stumbled. Then the anger of the Lord was aroused against Uzzah, and God struck him there for his error, (or irreverence), and he died there by the ark of God... David was afraid of the Lord that day; and he said, 'How can the ark of the Lord, (or the glory of the Lord), come to me? So David would not move the ark of the Lord with him into the city of David; but David took it aside into the house of Obed-Edom the Gittite... And the Lord blessed Obed-Edom and all his household."

- (2 Samuel 6: 6-11) -

The hour has come when God has called His people to be carriers of His glory. The scripture you have just read from 2 Samuel gives us a clear picture of the warnings and benefits of that calling. It's a new hour and many of us have been prepared for a greater measure, a much greater measure, of the new wine of God's Spirit. It doesn't take a rocket scientist to look around at the world we live in and know that a greater glory of God is desperately needed.

To be a carrier of God's glory, one of the most fundamental principles that must be present in our lives is deep reverence for who God really is. In the Bible this reverence is the fear of the Lord.

Let's look at the book of Acts once again and remember, this is after Jesus was crucified and raised from the dead! In other words, the dispensation of grace had come; the one we now live in!

"But a certain man named Ananias, with Saphira his wife, sold a Possession and kept the back part of the proceeds, his wife also being aware of it, and brought a certain part and laid it at the apostle's feet. But Peter said, 'Ananias, why has Satan filled your heart to lie to the Holy Spirit, and keep back part of the price of the land for yourself? While it remained, was it not your own? And after it was sold, was it not in your own control? Why have you conceived this thing in your heart? You have not lied to men but to God!' Then Ananias, hearing these words, fell down and breathed his last. So great fear came upon all those who heard these things..."

- (Acts 5: 1-5) –

## People of Power

"And through the hands of the apostles many signs and wonders were done among the people. And they were all with one accord in Solomon's Porch. Yet none of the rest dared join them, but the people esteemed them highly. And believers were increasingly added to the Lord, multitudes of both men and women so that they brought the sick out into the streets and laid them on beds and couches, that at least the shadow of Peter passing by might fall on some of them. Also a multitude gathered from the surrounding cities to Jerusalem bringing sick people and those who were tormented by unclean spirits, and they were all healed."

- (Acts 5: 12 - 16) -

Many have argued that the signs and wonders were only for the original apostles. However, notice in the above scripture where it is stated that, "yet none of the rest dared join them, but the people esteemed them highly. And believers were increasingly added to the Lord..." What was the difference between those who were added to the Lord and the apostles who were performing the signs and wonders? "None of the rest dared join them!"

Today, if you will hear His voice, God is daring you to join them! The definition of the word "dare" is to find the courage to take action, or to be adventurous.

Believe the Lord for the great adventure He has in store for you. Be not afraid of the dreams God has placed in your heart, for once refined He will use them with great power.

Many of you have been prepared. Now get ready to be, "esteemed highly." Where once the world looked down on the ministers and people of God, they now begin to look up.

## A New Season

September 11, 2001 forever changed the course of history. The day those two towers fell was the day disrespect for God and His people fell as well. Suddenly, people were flocking to churches and news networks were talking to ministers, all looking for answers. Granted, some of that faded shortly after, but that does not negate the fact that the "writing was on the wall." I say all of this to say that it was confirmation of a revelation the Lord gave to me a number of years ago...

I was approaching my second decade of pursuing God and was fasting, praying, and asking Him to please show me what the second decade of my life with Him would be like. He answered in a dream on about the twenty-first day of the fast.

In the dream, I found myself in a large and spacious room with a small group of people. Around the room itself were what seemed to be different workout stations. They were not like exercise stations, but rather a room full of different experiences. We, the people and I, followed an angel of the Lord to the first station. The station itself was under a bright light. I saw a pure white music stand placed at the foot of a hospital bed. That was it. The angel motioned for a young man standing next to me to partake of the experience, however he hesitated to do so. When he did, I immediately volunteered myself. At that, the angel motioned for me to partake.

As I stood before the music stand, I could hear the distant sound of worship music. Upon the music stand itself was a small scroll of paper. I decided to pick the paper up and when I did, instant pain shot throughout my entire being causing me to fall to my knees. Blood began to pour out from every part of my body. It was the most excruciating pain I had ever felt and yet, at the same time, the most cleansing feeling as well. I was experiencing it; I had the sense that I was feeling just an ounce of what Jesus experienced Himself when fastened to the cross. The pain and cleansing lasted for just a few minutes.

When it was over, I stood to my feet once and dropped the scroll upon the music stand. The moment it left my fingers, I was instantly clothed in a pure white robe of righteousness. It was made known to me that what I had just experienced was what I had been experiencing for the entire first ten years of my journey with God. Then it was time to go to the new season of experience.

I followed the angel of the Lord to the next station where a large stage stood about six feet off the ground. Upon the stage itself was a person dancing and shouting the high praises of God. Leading to the platform were a number of steps. I placed my feet upon the first step but knew that I had to wait for the person to complete the experience before I could partake myself. While waiting, I casually looked around and saw a marble plaque hanging from the side of the stage.

I instantly knew it was the title of the next season. There, wrtten in stone on the side of the exalted stage were the words...

### "Victory Over the Devil."

I woke up from the dream; I was excited, and for obvious reasons. However, I knew that the revelation was for more than just myself. I felt that it also spoke about the church, the body of Christ. The interpretation was clear. I myself, like the church, had just come through a season of pain and cleansing. A season of crucifixion. A season spent in intimate worship as we all laid upon God's hospital bed to be healed of our wounds. That was the first station, but the second station spoke of a much different experience. A new season.

I believe with all of my heart that the Church is about to enter into a season of great victory. That even the sounds of the music we sing will take on a whole new tone. A sound of high praise! It is a season where we will dance and shout like David did. Remember after the ark, or glory of the Lord, rested quietly and hidden, as it were, in the house of Obed-Edom? David had the privilege of bringing the glory into Jerusalem for all to see. In other words, it was time for God's glory to arise and the people of God to rejoice with high praises!!

"Now it was told to David, saying, 'The Lord has blessed the house of Obed-Edom and all that belongs to him, because of the ark of God!' So David went and brought up the ark of God from the house of Obed-Edom to the City of David with gladness.

And so it was, when those bearing the ark of the Lord had gone six paces, that he sacrificed oxen and fatted sheep. Then David danced before the Lord with all his might, and David was wearing a linen ephod. So David and all the house of Israel brought up the ark of the Lord with shouting and with the sound of the trumpet."

- (2 Samuel 6: 12-15) -

David, with reverence and the prescribed method of carrying the ark, entered Jerusalem with humility (God's way of doing things). The ark itself was then carried on the shoulders of the priests themselves rather than the undistinguished cart of an ox.

It is time for us, the people of God, to carry the glory on our own shoulders. No longer will God's glory rest upon the program of a corporate machine. Our shoulders are the ones God wants to rest upon, not our buildings and bank accounts. Yes, there will be those who will mock and think they can look down upon us from their lofty perches of pride, but they will soon be the minority. Be prepared for the hour to speak as David once spoke...

"Therefore, I will play music before the Lord... And will be more undignified than this, and will be humble in my own sight. But as for the maidservants of whom you have spoken, by them I will be held in honor."

- (2 Samuel 6: 21-22) -

Get ready to be "held in honor", for it is God's will to set His people upon a stage for all the world to see. Jesus Himself said...

"You are the light of the world. A city that is set on a hill cannot be hidden. Nor do they light a lamp and put it under a basket, but on a lamp stand, and it gives light to all who are in the house. Let your light so shine before men, that they may see your good works and glory your Father in heaven."

- (Matthew 5: 14-16) –

## Three, Two, One...

Cathy, myself, and all of Breath of the Almighty Ministries are no longer adrift upon the open sea. As it stands, we've been given a new vehicle to launch out with. A vehicle that has been properly covered as well) I might add.

Where once the creaky wooden planks of an ancient sailing ship echoed through the caverns of our questioning and often confusing journey, now are replaced with sounds of mighty rockets being filled with nitro fuel. The ice that once stood as bergs ready to gouge holes in the hull of the ship now serve only to keep the rocket cylinders cold until the time of takeoff. The hustle and bustle of anticipated excitement now replaces the humdrum of the laborious loading of cargo.

The oceans have been completely chartered and mapped by the former generations and thank God for the invaluable experience we can build upon. Where would the global positioning system be without the sextant? However, a new ceremony now replaces the breaking of champagne bottles on the bow.

Crowds still gather, and the excitement is still tangible. God's power and presence is still with us just as it has always been. However, greater power and more fire; greater heat and more light is about to be released through greater clouds of rolling glory just on the other side of the fullness of God's perfect timing... and His count down...

Whatever level you are at. Whatever step you are on in this journey with God. Whether you have yet to begin or whether you have been vigorously traveling, there is an appointed time for you as well. Your pursuit of Him has not and will not be in vain. The calling He has for you will never be unavailable. The countdown has never been changed. The count down is today! If you will hear His voice, it is today...

A call to pursue is for today!

Three...        Two...        One...


LAUNCH!!!

# Chapter 9

## A Kingdom Parable

"All these things spake Jesus unto the multitudes in Parables; and without a parable spake he not unto them: That it might be fulfilled which was spoken by the Prophet, saying, I will open my mouth in Parables; I will utter things which have been kept secret from the foundation of the world."

- (Matthew 13: 34-35) -

I believe that the Lord has moved upon my heart to write this book for the purpose of stirring up a hunger within people. Within all people... everywhere. To encourage them to pursue God and to pursue His calling upon their lives.

Perhaps you have been pursuing, or have at one time. Perhaps you have had the "dream" to fulfill your destiny, but now feel as though you've tried everything and are close to giving up. Maybe you have even tried and tried again and feel as though you've only failed time after time.

Perhaps you are those who have had the dream and somehow believe that it has completely died for one reason or another. If so, I offer this chapter to you. It is designed to minister to you, the dreamers. It's dedicated to those of you who, at one time, have dared to dream the impossible dream, but now believe that dreams are only fantasies and figments of the imagination. Suppose, just suppose, that the dream could live again.

Did you know that every dream has to die before it can truly live? God Himself once had a dream. His dream was to have His own family, but before that dream could become a reality it had to die as well. In fact, it died on a lonely tree just outside the city of Jerusalem. However, it was also just outside the city of Jerusalem that the dream lived once again!

This is a story, or rather a parable, that the Lord gave to me one day while I was diving down a busy freeway in Southern California. It was one of those times that the Holy Spirit filled the car unexpectedly. You know the ones! The kind that takes your breath away. More than once He has taken my breath away by the things He has said, because He may only speak one or two words, but He means volumes. "Let there be light," was certainly loaded with volumes was it not?

The story itself was actually inspired by an event that took place in my wife's life, and the Lord used that event to speak to me. Cathy had just completed the finishing touches on a beautiful gourmet meal for a friend of ours who also happened to be a mighty prophet of God as well. It was a richly decorated slice of salmon topped with capers in a white wine sauce; and it was cooked to perfection. The meal itself was actually a big sacrifice of time and money for our family, but she felt as though the Lord had put it upon her heart to do, so I told her that she should definitely do it.

However, just before it was time to take the salmon out of the oven, the glass dish that it was simmering in exploded, completely destroying the meal!

She instantly became upset, knowing that the Lord had moved upon her heart to make the sacrifice, but the Lord comforted her with these words...

"I told you to just create the meal for the prophet of God, not to deliver it."

The following story illustrates the volumes of which He spoke.

## The Sacrifice

There was once a young man who lived in a kingdom long ago. Although the young man was merely a peasant, his heart was much larger than his livelihood. One day, an impossible dream found its way into his aspiring heart; a dream that eventually became his passion for living.

The young man dreamed of one day visiting the majestic castle of the King to present to him the finest gift in all the realm, for he was a potter. He was the one that supplied the vessels to those who would purchase his wares for the purpose of retrieving water from the rivers and streams which flowed throughout the shire.

With his dream firmly planted in his heart, he set out to create the most beautiful vessel he possibly could. Every night, and into the wee hours of the morning, he would work on the vessel after his daily duties were completed. Sometimes only getting a few hours of rest. This continued for six long years as he tried over and over to get the gift just right, his dream ever-present with him.

Yes, he knew it to be an impossible dream for in that kingdom no one was allowed to see the King face to face. Legend had it that the King himself positioned his throne behind a large curtain, and never came out from behind it. The young man, along with every other citizen of the kingdom, knew that even rulers and nobles from other realms were not allowed beyond that curtain. In fact, they were told to leave the gifts in the courtroom where only the prince would receive them. Nevertheless, the young man's dream continued to live and exist beyond those mere facts.

More than once the young man let his tucked-away dream see the light of day, and every time he did the cruel mocking and the much snickering of other people sought to extinguish its flame. Many of the people knocked on the door of his pottery shop only to run away as he answered in a gesture of ill-will.

However, even through the torrents of shame, the dream lived on, and the young man's faith persisted. Until, at long last, he felt that he had finished the gift.

The vessel itself was beautifully shaped with handles and ornate decorations. Untold hours of work went into it. With confidence in the fact that he had created the best vessel ever, he gently placed the brown-clay pot beneath his work bench and covered it with a burlap cloth in hopes that one day it could be uncovered and presented.

That one day arrived when there came a peculiar knock on the door. The young potter could hear the hushed voices of the townspeople just outside so he didn't even bother to answer it because he thought they would only run away as they usually did. However, the knock persisted until reluctantly, the young man was compelled to answer. To his utter surprise, a herald of the King stood before him with a scroll in his hand. Unrolling the scroll, the herald proceeded to read the writing...

"You are hereby summoned to appear before his royal majesty in a mere three days from now, and are to present your gift in the courtrooms of the King."

As the herald returned to his horse, a slight smile slid its way across the mouth of the young man while the townspeople looked at him in awe and wonder.

Days later, the young man's lifelong dream became a reality.

Arriving at the castle upon a horse that trailed behind the herald, the young potter silently stared at the enormous marble gatehouse. Beyond it, the majestic white castle of the King. He could see waterfalls pouring out from beneath the foundational rock that created the rivers and streams that flowed throughout the entire realm. In the distance, he could see the source of that water; glorious snowcapped mountains that soared high into the sky where white clouds shrouded their peaks. It was a marvelous sight to behold. However, it was only the beginning for the young peasant.

As he entered the courtroom, his breath was slightly taken from him as the beauty of the place enveloped him like a fine morning mist... Then, he saw the curtain. "The legend is true!" he thought to himself as his legs became slightly weak around the middle joints. He was so dumbstruck that he nearly dropped the vessel that he had come all that way there to present. Never before had a mere peasant been found in such a fortuitous place... And, as the legend had stated, the prince and only son of the King stood before the curtain ready to receive his father's gift.

As the herald ushered the young man foreword, he approached with caution. Each step seemed to take longer as he made his way closer to the curtain and the prince. Finally, upon arrival he bowed his knee before the son of the King. "Is this your gift to the King?" asked the prince.

"Ye... yes sire. This is the one, replied the potter.

"Very well. Give it to me and I will present it to my father," stated the prince with authority.

The young man was just handing over the gift when his heart felt as if it would explode. He knew that it was then or never. He had to say something about his dream or lose it forever. With all the courage he could muster, he addressed the prince.

"Sire, forgive me, but it has always been my dream to present my gift to the King personally. If at all possible..."

"I'm sorry. No one is permitted beyond the veil," stated the prince again.

"But, but..."

"No... I will take it to him myself," interrupted the prince.

"But sire..."

"Young man, there is something you don't understand about my father," the prince finally stated with finality.

With that, the young potter bowed his head in silence and proceeded to lift the vessel in humble submission. It was then that the unthinkable happened. The vessel slipped from his hands!

Time itself seemed to slow to a crawl as he watched it fall in utter shock and horror. Worse still was the crashing sound it made as it shattered upon the unforgiving marble floor.

Life seemed to drain from his face as his dream lay shattered into hundreds of fragments at the prince's feet. The pause that followed hung in the air like a puff of smoke that even wind could not possibly drive away.

Nearby, the guards broke the silence as they moved to clean up the mess but were soon waived off by the unaffected prince. The peasant potter dared not lift his head and found himself frozen in time not sure what to do, how to react, or how to even breathe. A slightly sickening feeling began to creep into his freshly lacerated heart. Bitter anger gnashed its teeth as it tried to enter the wound, but the humble potter refused to give in to its slithery voice... Especially in the presence of royalty.

"You've broken your vessel," the prince replied rather warmly.

"I'm such a fool! ", was the young man's involuntary response as he instantly moved to clean up the mess.

"Don't touch a thing! This is exactly what I've been waiting for," retorted the prince.

The statement was shocking!

However, as shocking as it was, nothing could prepare the young man for what happened next. Right there in front of the peasant and in the presence of the surrounding guards, the prince and son of the King stooped down and began to gather the shards of pottery together one methodical piece at a time.

"I mean no disrespect sire, but please let me do that myself," pleaded the potter. I should be the one on my hands and knees. I'm the one who let the gift fall." As the prince continued to gather the pieces together, he spoke with an authoritative tone. "I know you don't understand why I am doing this now, but you will in time."

"Please sire, you make me feel ashamed." At that precise moment, the bitter anger that lurked just outside the wound in the potter's heart because of his own mistake breached the wall and stormed the gates.

"No, I will not see you made a fool for my mistake!" As he rushed toward the stooped down prince the peasant was seized by the nearby guards and held tightly as the prince stood to his feet.

Finally, breaking down in tears, the peasant potter cried out. "Oh, sire... If only I could have carried the vessel straight to the King myself, this never would have happened."

"It simply was not possible at this time..." replied the prince and continued picking up the pieces of the potter's dream once again.

The young man felt as if he would explode with motion. Sensing trouble, the prince motioned for the guards to remove the young peasant from the castle.

Broken shards near powdery piles of dust, coupled with the prince himself, stooped down once again, were the last ghastly images the young potter saw of his lifelong dream, and consequently, the last time he set foot in the courtroom of the great King.

Until...

One day, months later, the young man heard a knock at the door of his pottery shop. He didn't answer the door very much anymore and would only go outside in those wee hours of the morning when he used to work on his dream. The depression even began to eat away at his health. As the knock persisted, the frail and emaciated young man finally made his way to the door. Opening it with trepidation, he peered out through the tiny opening which he barely allowed. It was one of the greatest mistakes of his life... Or so he thought at the time.

There, standing before the door, was the same herald that had visited him months earlier. Again, he had a scroll rolled up in his hand. As the herald unrolled the scroll to read the young potter slammed the door of the shop, turned away from it, and fell back against it.

Sliding down to his knees, he let his face fall into his hands. "What is the King trying to do to me?" thought the young man to himself.

Outside, he could hear the herald mounting his horse to leave. Inside, a war raged upon the sea of his own emotions which had previously lain deathly still. Finally, he mustered the strength to stand and opened the door.

The herald of the King had just mounted his horse when he heard the door open one more time. He was actually shocked to see the condition that the young man had succumbed to. Rather than formally reading the scroll, he rather warmly asked the young peasant to join him on a journey to the castle and simply stated, "You are to appear before the King."

The ride to the castle was a rigorous one for the young man, not because the road was rough, but because of the pain that still lingered like a thick soupy fog. Finally, when they arrived, the herald walked the potter through the gates and to the entrance of the majestic courtroom. Once inside, the young man was on his own.

Again he saw the beauty of the room and the large curtain at the end of it, but somehow it had all lost its luster. As usual, the prince was standing at the end of the room, waiting. With even more trepidation, the young man approached and slightly bowed.

"Sire," he stated somewhat coldly.

"Did I not tell you that there was something about my father which you did not understand?" asked the prince.

"Yes, sire you did," replied the peasant.

"Today, you will be the first outsider to enter beyond this veil, and I will take you there myself."

Pulling back the folds of the heavy curtain, the prince escorted the young peasant into the throne room of the great King. Either out of reverence, or because he simply could not, the young man refused to allow his eyes to wander too high above the ground and kept his head held low. What he could see, however, was shocking to him. The room itself was the most beautiful place that he had ever even imagined.

He found himself standing upon a pathway made of pure gold. So refined was it, that it seemed to be transparent. Diamonds, rubies, emeralds, and many other precious stones lined the pathway on both sides. Candlelight and a soft mist seemed to blanket the room with warmth. Half trying to shield his eyes from the light, and half trying to cover tears that were threatening to escape their pent-up cages, the young man placed his hand above his brow so that he could see more clearly. When he did, he was stunned at what he saw:

Gifts and treasures of all sorts sat upon pillars and pedestals all around the room. However, upon one of the pillars and in the center of the room was a vessel strangely shaped in a familiar way and was adorned with gold and diamonds. To the young man, it looked just like the pot he had made himself. "But that's impossible, this one's decorated with gold and diamonds. Mine was broken to pieces," thought the young man to himself.

Suddenly, as if knowing what the young man was thinking, the prince spoke. "This is what has become of your gift to the King.

"I don't understand. That's my gift?" asked the potter.

Again, the prince spoke. "This is what you did not understand. You see the King, my father, has instructed me to present to him a gift only from my hands, and my hands alone... That is, unless it has been broken first."

The young potter stood in utter silence as the prince continued.

"You have discovered something about my father that no one else has before, and for that you have been granted the privilege to be the first to come beyond this veil with me. You see, it's very simple. What you brought to the King was a sacrifice. It was a sacrifice of time, talent, and countless hours of effort. It was your dream. However, all of your work and, consequently, your dream was shattered that day you dropped it on the floor in my presence... And the day you dropped it on the floor in my presence was the day it became one of the greatest gifts my father has ever received.

"I don't understand..." replied the peasant.

"You see, it was a broken sacrifice... And nothing gives my father greater pleasure than to repair that which has been broken!"

## The Veil of Decision

A herald of the King stands before you too at this moment, with a scroll unrolled in his hand. Do you want to know what the scroll says? It reads...

The veil has been pulled back and the Son has welcomed you inside. He has given you the greatest gift of all. In fact, it's the finest gift in all the realm. It's called access. An entrance has been supplied for you to the Presence of His Father, and yours...

Make the decision to pursue Him.

Make that decision today!

Simply ask Jesus into your heart.

Ask him to forgive you of your sins.

It's that easy because...

A Call to Pursue

He has loved you with an everlasting love and He has called you unto Himself.

He still has a calling upon your life as well... And, to be quite honest,

It's a call to pursue!

# Epilog

The words that I have written in this book have been quite humbling for my wife and I to reveal. However, on the day that I was water baptized many years ago I was handed two simple items as I emerged from the pool. I still have no clue as to who it was that handed them to me. One item was a clean towel and the other was a note written on a tiny piece of paper. Part of that note read: "Be willing to be vulnerable and transparent, for My power will manifest most dramatically when you bare your heart to others."

I pray that this has been the case.

Although Cathy and I are ministers that God has revealed Himself to in a powerful way, we are merely human as well. Human through and through. Every novel, every play, and every film... Every story has its main characters that are usually its heroes as well.

Although my wife and I are the main characters of the story you have just read, we are certainly not its heroes.

The only hero of this story is the Lord Jesus Himself. It was His love, His patience, His long-suffering, and His grace that carried us, and still does today.

When all is said and done and there is a new Heaven and a new Earth, you and I will not have been the ones proved to be strong. It will have been our weaknesses that prove God alone is the strongest of all. He alone will have been the one to have carried the day!

I have written these things so that you may glean not only from our strong points, but more importantly, from our weak ones. May you continue your own journeys with God in His strength and in the power of His might. May He always be with you, not only as He has always been, but as He ever shall be.

Amen!

God be with you,

Paul Lawrence

Paul Lawrence's next book:

"The Firefighters Guide to the Fire of God"

Will be available soon!


At BreathofAlmighty.org

ChoicePublications.org


Amazon, Barnes & Noble, and Booksellers
around the globe!

www.ingramcontent.com/pod-product-compliance
Lightning Source LLC
Chambersburg PA
CBHW020254130626
46549CB00005B/2204